DYNASTY

CHRISTINA OXENBERG

DYNASTY

A TRUE STORY

QUARTET BOOKS

First published in Great Britain by Quartet Books Limited in 2018
A member of the Namara Group
27 Goodge Street, London, W1T 2LD

A catalogue record for this book is available from the British Library.

ISBN 9780704374485

Text design and typesetting by Tetragon, London
Printed and bound in Great Britain by TJ International Ltd, Padstow, Cornwall

THIS BOOK IS DEDICATED TO

Karageorge
and all his descendants

AND TO

My beautiful, courageous and ageless mother
HRH Princess Elizabeth of Yugoslavia

CONTENTS

The Princess Myth   xi

Why Serbia Now?   xiii

1   HRH Prince Paul of Serbia: Part I   1

2   HRH Princess Olga of Greece and Denmark   26

3   HRH Prince Paul of Yugoslavia: Part II   57

4   Karageorge   80

5   HSH Prince Alexander I of Serbia   114

6   HRH Prince Arsen of Yugoslavia   127

7   Princess and Countess
    Aurora Demidoff di San Donato   139

8   HM King Peter I of the Serbs, Croats and Slovenes   150

9   HM King Alexander I of Yugoslavia   167

10 HM King Peter II of Yugoslavia and
    HRH Crown Prince Alexander of Yugoslavia   179

Epilogue   211

Acknowledgements   221

Author's Note   225

'It is easy for me to be grand with our well-experienced army and vast financial means, but down in the south, in the Balkans, there is a marshal who has arisen from the simple peasant folk, and who gathered his sheepherders, and without sophisticated weapons with just the small cannons, shook the foundation of the almighty Ottoman Empire thus freeing his enslaved people. That is Karageorge; to him goes all the glory of being the greatest general.'

NAPOLEON BONAPARTE

THE PRINCESS MYTH

GIRLS ALL OVER THE WORLD DREAM OF BEING A PRINCESS. Not unreasonably, they imagine wearing the finest frocks and being squired by the most desirable bachelors; being pampered in palaces of marble; living lives of unimaginable splendour. Why not such a dream, indeed? They would be wise, however, to beware and never forget that beneath the surface are veins of boiling vengeance. Behind the glory lie heaps of mutilated bodies, rival brothers hanged or hacked to death, tremulous fathers mercilessly shot. The founder of the Serbian Karageorgević dynasty met with a grisly end – decapitated – his head sent to the Grand Sultan in Constantinople. All this was so that one day Serbia's children might exist in tranquillity, free of repression by Turks or their vassals, and with the gory past politely swept aside. From a mountain geyser spout the first droplets of a widening river of descendants eventually emptying into the sea, the sea of civilized life where they could become noble patrons of the arts and aesthetes.

I look at footage of King Alexander I, driving through Marseilles in 1934. He is dapper, wearing formal military dress in an open car. He is smiling at the thronging crowds that welcome his official visit. He is visibly pleased. Then he is shot dead instantly, and his head slumps sideways, blood oozing down his jaw. It was shocking to me to watch this. What a way to meet a relative.

How does such a dynasty begin?

Christina Oxenberg, 2018

WHY SERBIA NOW?

DESPITE MY RESEARCH INTO THE STORY OF MY SERBIAN Karageorgević family, while I have nothing but respect and admiration for all they accomplished, my intention is not to dwell on these last 200 years. I doff my hat, I reverentially remember them and restore their stories here as best I can. But my objective is forward-looking. My goal and my hope is to carry on their name so that my generation and the others of the Karageorgević clan can continue the tradition of humbly serving the country of Serbia, helping the needy and promoting the sciences and the arts, of which there are an abundance. My vision is for the present and for the future. I curtsy respectfully to my ancestors, and I stride proudly forward hand in hand with the Serbia of the twenty-first century. That is my most sincere wish and intention. Please join me on this quest.

As is the way with my life, unexpected turns present themselves and switch my direction, sending me down unpredictable routes. So why Serbia now? I have decided I will spend my remaining years studying my mother's side of things, this Serbian side. Then, surely, I shall be done! I would never have decided this in any strategic way. Rather, a trove of good luck fell into my lap; glittering gifts that include a crypt of my own at the family mausoleum in Topola, central Serbia, a land of mountains and forests thick with poplar trees and the sweetest air. When the time comes I will be all dressed up and I will have somewhere to go.

By birth I am an American, born on the Upper East Side of New York City. All my life I attributed much of my personality to this single fact. Gradually, I learned the same truths as do so many children and grandchildren of immigrants born in the States – that there is a past, there is a story, but everyone has done their best to forget it, to eradicate it. It is typical of an American, somewhere around middle age, as I am now, to look up from gazing at the ground beneath one's feet, after years of sifting the soil and hoping for local answers only, to look up, blinking at the brightness and the hugeness of the world and to begin a search for explanations on a horizon that goes beyond the world as one sees it. The world of the past. It is equally typical for an American to begin this enquiry by asking questions of parents and grandparents only to discover they have chosen to forget everything. In many cases the grandparents, if they were the first to board those rickety ships and cross the fierce unforgiving Atlantic Ocean, might not have learned English and cannot even communicate with their grandchildren. They will deny their religious heritage. They will obscure their origins. The only thing they might hold dear are recipes for favourite foods. This 'origin-washing' is so thorough – all information so bleached – that the seeker is likely to give up the quest before starting. As my friend the professional photographer Leigh Honey Vogel says, 'If I tried to research my family roots, I'd hit a dead end somewhere in the Bronx and that would be the end of it.'

I am well aware that my situation is unique and am very grateful because instead of a wilfully reluctant relative who claims airily, 'We come from somewhere in Russia, it's all long ago now, don't ask questions. Have some more soup,' I can fire up the Internet and research my family – at least, my mother's side of the family. This is a luxury for an American, and I have only just begun to take advantage of it.

What do you think an American is? I ask this because when I travel abroad I am often privy to hostility and judgements. Do you think they sprang out of the ground? I will tell you: they are the descendants of people from all over the world, they are your ancestors' lost grandchildren and they do not know who they are. They are rootless. They have no personal identity. From house to house they have no bond. That is why they obsessively ask each other, 'Where are you from?' and inevitably the answer is the name of a town and a state. But the real question is far subtler than they even realize, and the correct answer is not known to them. The truth is they have no idea where they are from or who they are, so their identities are fashioned on the spot – and they create themselves. America is the great experiment and many have thrived from this experiment. However, in the eyes of some this is an experiment that has not fared so well.

Having never been to Serbia in my entire life, I travelled to Belgrade to attend a party in the summer of 2014. Sure, it is a long way to go for a fiesta but the circumstances were appealing to me. The soirée was in honour of the restoration of a property taken from my Serbian family after they were thrown out of the country all those years ago. Obviously, the family lost far more than just property – they lost their homeland. We have all been wandering ever since.

When, in 2014, the Serbian government restored ownership of this property to my mother and her brother Prince Alexander, it was for us a very big deal; the first true welcome home after half a century of exile and death threats. To me, along with many family members, this was a reason to celebrate. Karageorgević cousins from all over the world converged in Belgrade in the summer of 2014; we bonded instantly, for the first time and for the same cause. We recognized one another immediately, because we all look exactly alike. This was an exhilarating experience.

I am half-Serbian. I was born in New York City and raised in England, resulting in a mishmash of an accent. Americans assume I am British but I don't have a drop of British blood and all my life, in America anyway, I have had to explain that despite my strong accent, I am not a Brit! A real Brit, however, never thinks I am one of them. Instead they tell me my accent is an American one they can understand. Consequently, I have never felt that I belonged anywhere and this feeling has been reinforced by the reactions of others. Countless times an American has asked me, 'Where are you from?' When I reply, 'New York City,' they respond by laughingly declaring, 'No way! Not with that accent!'

It is quite something to be scolded by a complete stranger over my own origins, and it has repeatedly reinforced my sense of rootlessness. After all, I know where I was born – New York City – yet no one believes me, and I know I am half-Serbian although I had not visited the country until recently. My personal tapestry is threadbare, nearly see-through. The bad side of this is that it has made for a lifetime of feeling alien wherever I am, while the good side is that I can feel comfortable anywhere. But the proof of the deep-rootedness of this confusion is that I have never lived anywhere for very long, and I have never returned to any place I have lived. I have only ever moved forward, though now that I examine things I see it was never forward, but rather lateral.

This investigation into Serbia and the story of the Karageorgević family is indeed, finally, a step forward.

It has been my experience through the years to be asked a question that has increasingly shredded my already minimal patience, mostly because it is boring to have repeated this conversation ad infinitum. Here's exactly how it goes; picture a smoky, loud bar:

'Where are you from?'

'I'm from New York.'

'No you're not!'

'You know better?'

'But you have an accent!'

'You must be a musician with such a fine ear.'

'Australia?'

'No.'

'South Africa?'

'No.'

'Canada?'

'No.'

'New Zealand?'

'No.'

'OK, I give up. Where are you from?'

'I already told you an hour ago, I'm from New York. Born in New York City. Would you like to see my ID?'

'But you have an accent?'

'I'm a combination of Brooklyn Jew and Serbian princess.'

'What?'

'What?'

'What?'

'What?'

'So, where is Siberia?'

But on a deeper level this excruciating and predictable exchange has bothered me because it reminds me of my very real dislocation. Why am I never welcomed? Why am I always challenged to prove my identity?

When I showed my passport to the customs man at Nikola Tesla Airport outside Belgrade he looked up and said to me, 'I know who you are.'

I was shocked. This has never happened to me before. I asked him, 'Why don't you say welcome home?'

He said, 'Welcome home!'

That was the beginning of this new life for me.

When I told Serbs it was my first trip to the fatherland they said, 'What took you so long?' I hesitantly replied, 'Politics?', but I had to wonder, and I realized I had no idea. I have felt rootless all my life. Partly I blame my sensibilities on knowing about my family's harsh punishment, and I did not want to forgive a country that had so brutally wounded people dear to me. I felt a great deal of ambivalence towards Serbia, which is why it was not a country I had any desire to visit as a tourist. I waited a long time for a good reason, and along came this party. It seemed to fit. I bought myself a round-trip ticket for a five-day stay.

My initial concerns were petty, such as how I would get to the party and would my dress be crushed from so long in a suitcase, and if I could learn a couple of Serbian words to toss around. My first twenty-four hours were blearily devoted to sleeping in the lovely, modern hotel at the centre of Belgrade, and lots of room service. Then the *pièce de résistance* – the party; it was fabulous and well worth travelling a thousand hours for. I was very glad

I went. With me was the former US diplomat Henry Bisharat and Rasko Aksentijević, my first ever real live Serb friend whom I happen to know from my life in Key West, Florida.

Rasko was by chance in Belgrade at the same time as I, so the three of us attended the party and had a wonderful evening, each from our own perspective. I saw people across the room, strangers effectively, but I knew who they were because our faces are all the same with these huge, intense, dark eyes. I crossed the room and time after time I said, 'You must be a Karageorgević!' Invariably they would be and we would introduce ourselves, untangling the complications of dead uncles and aunts and grandparents who were cousins, and it was with raucous delight that we found one another. I have never experienced so many family members before and it was an intense pleasure. What I have known is being a peripheral member of someone else's family, a welcome guest of sorts, but nothing much closer than that. I have always felt acutely the chilly separation and observed the difference between my connection and those of others; they were much closer and more intimate. I have never been invited in, never asked to step inside anyone else's circle. I have never spoken about this, but I have felt it.

In the case of the night at Villa Olga, we cousins had never so much as heard of one another's existence and yet we could spot one another in the crowd. We came together like homing pigeons, quite naturally, and I believe we will not lose touch. This was a turning point for all of us, long overdue and much needed. Being in Serbia was almost more than I could comprehend at the time. At that party we were all reacting out of gut instinct, some sort of irrefutable genetic mode. It was not until I returned to America after my five-day visit that the significance began to gel, and I started to realize I was done with America for now. I wanted to be in Serbia. I was hooked.

The day after the party, my friend Rasko insisted on showing me Belgrade. Rasko is from the city of Kragujevac, the largest city in the district of Šumadija. Rasko is naturally an historian and he gave me a thorough tour of Belgrade. I would point at a good-looking building and ask, 'Can I live there?' and he would say, 'That is the Students' Cultural Center.' I loved everything I saw. I started to think about needing to stay longer. All day long I was introduced to my ancestors; one statue, one monument and one building at a time. The significance impressed me profoundly and I started to think about wanting a lot more time there.

My cousins, Crown Prince Alexander and Crown Princess Katherine, were out of town the week I was visiting, but they very kindly arranged for me to visit the royal palaces at Dedinje, and this was scheduled for the afternoon. I took Henry and Rasko with me and as soon as the car made its way past the tall gates manned by guards with guns, and we wound up in driveways surrounded by enormous pine trees and sweet-smelling air, we were all hushed. Henry and Rasko took endless photos while I, still in my flip-flops, gaped at objects and rooms I had heard about since I was a child, images of mythical proportions to me. I knew about the room where my mother was born, I had heard about it all my life.

My mother's life was a confluence of misdirection. She was born in a palace. She had her own bodyguard. She was the little princess. When she was four years old, an age where one is cognizant, her parents' lives became chaotic, and she and her nurse were swept up in this. Her bodyguard had to stay behind in a changing Serbia. He would be imprisoned for this service he performed for my family. He would be punished by the new regime, one of many of Tito's casualties, but my mother would not know about that. She was a tiny child and she would have been stunned into some sort of trance as the family were suddenly forced to escape, with changing landscapes and elements of terror in the air. She would have realized things were very different when suddenly they were all living in Africa and she was offered a mongoose for a pet, which she liked and named. But life as she had known it was over forever, even if it would be many years before she could hope to understand what the hell had happened.

During my childhood, which was mostly spent in London, I often heard my mother speak about the house she was born in: Beli Dvor. These were our first Serbian words, even though it was merely a name to us. It would be fifty years before I thought to ask if that name even meant anything, and as it turns out it does: White Palace. How about that! I knew about this palace, and I knew there was a room where my mother was born. It must have meant a lot to her because otherwise she would not have mentioned it. But she spoke of it frequently enough so that when I saw it with my own eyes I was stunned into silence. Chills ran through me. I stopped – poised on the doorstep – and stared; stared at the quiet blues of the room. It was enormously significant to me, dredging up so many emotions. I had never entered this room in my life and yet I knew it intimately. It was a part of my own childhood as much as my mother's because she spoke of it. Simple words keep the past alive. As Nikos Kazantzakis said, you keep the dead alive by speaking of them.

When you walk into Beli Dvor you enter first a hall of quiet cream marble with mirrors and flags, and then a large square foyer topped by glass skylights and flanked with sweeping stairs to the second floor, visible as a balcony, perhaps from which to make a very spectacular entrance in formal attire. The focal point of the room is a fireplace over which hangs a large portrait of King Peter I. The floor is made of diamonds of black and white marble, each stone the size of an elephant's footprint and the tall walls are hung with portraits of ancestors, including my beautiful grandmother Princess Olga. In this painting – which I had never seen before – she is young, in her twenties, in a green dress to match her eyes, and she wears no jewellery whatsoever, a modest representation of an otherwise grand lady. Tucked beneath one of the sweeping staircases is a black grand piano and I can easily picture my grandfather sitting there, lost in the sounds of beauty echoing off the marble floor and the glass ceiling, and surrounded by the paintings on the walls – the Tintorettos and Canelettos – all of which he had painstakingly and lovingly sought out and bought. How could he know as he played that piano, probably Chopin's nocturnes, that everything would be ripped away from him one day?

Henry photographed methodically and Rasko went wild when he saw one of the cannons – an item he knew from history lessons as a child. And I, well, I looked at everything, and sucked it in. It floored me because everything was drenched in significance. There are men on the palace staff who care for the house, and in the winter they move the paintings around so they do not gather mould. I shook their hands and told them on behalf of my grandfather I was grateful.

On that first voyage to the homeland I had blinked and it was Friday, my last day, but my flight out wasn't until the evening so I decided to visit my Facebook friend Zeljka Milanović if only just to prove her wrong – for years she had been telling me she didn't believe I would ever show up. Honestly, I didn't know when it would happen, though I was certain it would one day. I was just waiting for the right time and here it was. 'Operation Serbia' so far was fairly threadbare – attend a party, if possible visit my friend, and then get home and blog about it. When I got there, the blinkers quickly fell away and my eyes opened wide. My curiosity proliferated exponentially, in fast-forward, and I wanted to stay.

Friday morning Henry and I hired a car and driver and motored off to meet my Internet friend, a girl I've been writing to for years. The drive took about an hour, past rolling green fields and hay barns and distant hills and trees filled with magpies. We gradually drove up into mountains dark with poplar forests and blasted with beams of sunlight. I found it beautiful, and I began to consider I still had no clue where Zeljka lived, even which direction from Belgrade we were pointed.

Over the years I have always promised that one day I would come to her home town; I would show up and say hello for real. The years passed and even though my plans dragged and changed, she was very tolerant and understanding; but she also let me know she didn't really expect me to ever show up. On my side, it has been a fraught emotional conveyor belt and getting me there, slowly – very slowly – was like moulding molten pig iron into something tangible. But I did show up and, as planned, we met at Oplenac. We spotted each other and after the tiniest hesitation we ran and hugged and said hello. When we met up Zeljka was slightly remote, visibly dazed and maybe even a little soused. She told me she got so nervous she almost didn't show up. 'Why?' I asked her. Because she never expected this to happen! And then we laughed and I gave her another hug and we walked and talked. Zeljka's English is excellent and she writes to me in long paragraphs. Shamefully, my Serbian was non-existent.

Zeljka is smart. She is a philosopher and she is funny. In our years of writing to each other she told me more than once that when Prince Tomislav lived nearby they took long walks in the gorgeous, sweet-smelling poplar forest. I knew a Prince Tomislav from my childhood in England, but I never really understood how we were related. Most of my childhood was so confusing to me I just gave up trying to understand it. I remember Tomislav as a looming figure with frightening, angular cheekbones, but equally I remember his tenderness and warmth. I remember liking him and I remember his daughter, Katerina. Equally I remember being confused that he was from the murky Serbian side and yet he lived in Kent, southern England, on a farm. I remember him wearing muddy Wellington boots. It made no sense to me. My memories are faded sepia tones and sometimes double exposed. My life never really became any less bewildering and many people were lost along the way. Now, however, many of them or their descendants are starting to show up.

I was never entirely sure if Zeljka and I were referring to the same Tomislav, because it didn't make any sense to me. How had he had been in both of our lives? I just didn't get it. And there was the matter of the family crypt, Oplenac, which Zeljka regularly visits. She was the one to explain to me that it was a mausoleum for the Karageorgević family, with room for me! She told me it was not in her village but nearby. For the most part I didn't know where the hell I was. It was as if I'd been spun around and let loose in zero gravity.

Then she asked, 'Want to see the crypt?' This was my first introduction to many relatives, some I had never heard of before like Kleopatra! Then there are those I miss, such as my grandparents. The tears began to burst free from somewhere deep in my heart and I melted. 'Wanna see the family museum? You know Karageorge was from here,' Zeljka told me. I had to confess I had no idea. She took me to the crypt, to the museum, to the King's winery, where I was given a box of bottles. 'You know,' Zeljka told me, 'The Šumadija district is Karageorge land. This is your home. Look, your name is on the family tree.' Sure enough my name was there, printed on a poster hanging on the wall at the entrance to the museum. There I was, in a country I had never visited before, far from anywhere I had ever been. On the wall. It was profound.

The family crypt is under Oplenac, a huge, imposing mosaic church of Byzantine excess and splendour. Zeljka sat outside on a bench. She said she'd smoke a cigarette and let me have time to myself in there. 'Go on,' she said, 'I'll be right here. You need to experience that by yourself.' In the crypt a guide introduced me, one deceased family member at a time, to my Serbian background. I discovered I had known next to nothing, or what I did know was wrong. This learning experience felt like entering an alternative universe. It turned out I didn't even know the head of the family's name, let alone what he was famous for, or who his descendants were, or how we were all related.

I had heard of Karageorge, the founder of the dynasty, except it turned out most of what I thought I knew was incorrect. I did not know his real name was George Petrović. Loosely, he grew up in eighteenth-century feudal Serbia and developed a reputation for his lack of regard for authority. His enemies derided him as swarthy – using the Turkish word for 'black' ('kara') – and they nicknamed him Black George, or Kara

George. Somehow the backhanded compliment stuck and he became Karageorge. Descendants maintained the name as Karageorgević, and so began the House of Karageorgević, Serbia's royal family.

In the Karageorgević museum I saw Karageorge's clothes, and everything from his scythes to his swords and guns. I heard tales of his ruthlessness, his uncompromising positions, his military brilliance and his overbearing side during times of peace. He was designed for war. Stories of murdering fathers and brothers piqued my curiosity further. Although I had not known any of this, I liked the sound of it. I liked the lack of hypocrisy. I felt intense pride for this man and all he had done; the people of Šumadija still revere him. His image hangs on every wall in town. To be there as his representative was a heady honour.

Our final stop was the bar where Zeljka works because no one there believed we are friends. For years she told them we are friends and they told her she is a crazy drunk, so I had to go show myself. A portrait of Karageorge hung on the wall of this establishment. I pointed at it, placed a hand on my heart and gave the owner a smile and a nod. It doesn't hurt that I happen to look rather exactly like this great Karageorge, just a smaller version. The proprietor was palpably dazed, though not more dazed than I already was, filled to the brim with so much new information, such an overload of new concepts. When I was told Karageorge killed a lot of people I was the opposite of horrified. In so many ways, I thought I felt a connection.

Guiltily and secretly I've long suspected that if I was a man I would be in prison for murder charges. I was told Karageorge ate very simply, as do I, and again I felt a connection. He was unpretentious, not interested in titles nor in medals. I feel the same.

He was brave and principled and motivated by righteousness, and rightly or wrongly I see myself that way too.

Gradually I began to understand why Tomislav had moved to this central Serbian village of Topola in 1991, from Kent in England. This was not the middle of nowhere, some place he had come to hide. This was home. England was exile. I was born in New York City and raised in England, and brought up hearing and speaking a dozen European languages; everything but Serbian. All of us Karageorgević cousins grew up all over the world – connections lost.

Zeljka was Tomislav's walking companion. Oddly this girl was our connection, although it had not sunk in how they were friends or why they took their walks until I went to Topola and saw this village, where Zeljka lives, and where my family is from. I had come to this town to have lunch with my girlfriend; we ate in the lobby of the restaurant of the only hotel in town. Gradually it sank in that Zeljka was one of my people. By virtue of visiting her I had stumbled upon the mouth of the river of the Karageorgević dynasty. I am ashamed to admit it was by happy accident I went home.

For the first time in my life I became curious. Who was this Karageorge? Who was this ruthless killer, liberator and founder of the country? It was time to have a look. I started to think about where I was heading with my life and I suddenly realized I had just arrived, on so many levels. All this opened up more questions. On the last day of the short trip I finally felt it all and I cried so much. Tears of relief; an amazing sensation. I felt I knew who I might be, after so long and so many questions, and so many moves. I already knew I would return soon because there was just so much still to discover.

I wanted to learn about George Petrović, the founder of modern Serbia. This is a story known to all Serbs, taught to them in elementary school. With the transfixed stupor that comes from staring at oneself in a mirror, the closer I examined my Slavic background the more infinitesimal details came into view, and layers of stories unfurled.

After that first journey I returned to my home in Key West, knowing my life there was decidedly altered. It was no longer the end of the line for me, but merely another scenic lookout on the road to somewhere. I had fallen in love with Serbia. I was hooked. I immediately made plans to return and to learn about Serbia and my Serbian family history. The entire journey back to America I cried and cried and cried, not from unhappiness – far from it – more like from a sense of relief; cleansing saline tears washing away years of uncertainty. Those tears floated me down-river from a place of stagnation to a new landscape. My future.

I knew my grandfather and my grandmother intimately, and while I was raised on random mentions of this land named Serbia, it was all as indistinct as any fairy tale. My only direct connection was to my grandparents. I was too young to eye them critically, but I was not so young that I could not respect their graciousness and impeccable good manners, applaud their sense of humour and love them for the warm, kind people they chose to be. All that I have learned about them, in this research, has only deepened my profound esteem for them. They shielded all of us, their grandchildren, from the hardships they endured. We knew nothing but love and tenderness from them. For this I thank them, redouble my admiration of them and humbly pray to do them justice in the pages of this book.

HRH Prince Paul of Serbia: Part I

27 April 1893 – 14 September 1976

WHEN I THINK OF MY GRANDFATHER I SEE HIM IN SUITS OF tweed, his neck wrapped in scarves and a hat covering his freckled yet otherwise balding head. He is walking in the park of Villa Demidoff in Tuscany, Italy, pacing slowly along to the syncopations of his walking stick. This Italian house and grounds were a comfortable, safe place where he passed the summers of his youth and old age. He would inherit this marvellous jewel after the death of a favourite Russian relative – Aunt Moina – in 1955.

My grandfather's Aunt Moina was his mother's sister: Maria Pavlovna Demidoff, Princess di San Donato (1877–1955) wife of Prince Semyon Semyonovich Abamelek-Lazarev (1857–1916). It was through Aunt Moina that Paul received not only much-needed emotional support but also an introduction to the finer things and eventually an inheritance to a most splendid fortune.

This villa was a home Paul cherished and knew intimately from many visits to his aunt since his early childhood. It was therefore fitting he should be the recipient of this stately structure, already filled with priceless treasures of paintings and antiques, from a family member to whom he was emotionally attached and to whom he owed far more than this villa with all its worldly goods. It was love he learned from her, and a few others like her; she showed up throughout his chilly childhood and graced him with the nurturing warmth of concern and affection. Although, sadly, by 1969 he would be obliged to sell the grand estate, as it was unmanageably large and too expensive to run, he had her in his heart until his last days on Earth. She was one of those many angels who fluttered through his otherwise stern and cold existence.

The Villa Demidoff was a building in the Italianate style of wide, smooth, dark terracotta walls and tall, elegant windows flanked by dark green shutters, the second story encircled by graceful balconies. The garden surrounding this house was really a park – it was immense – and inside were wide corridors, endless rooms and secret passageways. The owners of today's McMansions in California know the number of rooms in their house and proudly recount such trivia, but in my grandfather's time no one counted rooms or would consider evaluating a true mansion in terms of the number of rooms, or any such mundane issues. There were rooms we never even entered, servants' quarters we could not have located on an architectural map. A different world to today I understand, but none of us, my grandfather included, knew this yet.

Rain or shine, after lunch, my grandfather would lead the way, walking slowly with his cane and his formal suits and always a hat, as well as an umbrella if there was rain. We may have called it a garden but it was enormous and the exterior walls were further than the eye could see. He would lead the way, slowly and methodically, while his six grandchildren ran around him, flitting down wide, sandy, pebbled paths bordered by 100-year-old trees. Play was encouraged; imagination was inspired, ignited. As we strolled, he told us stories to try and make us laugh or sometimes scary stories accompanied by terrifying grimaces to make us shriek with panic and run off.

A favourite activity was to walk down paths to a leafy, tufted area of the garden with a giant grey stone statue beside a pond of huge white lilies. To us this was a favourite toy. Here we played in the hollow oversized statue of a man crouched in front of the pond, home to floating white lily petals and their vast bright-green pads where patient frogs squatted, waiting on meals of insects. This statue, known as the *Appennino*, is of a man the size of a modest cottage, with a door at the base of his spine. My grandfather would usher us through this door and carefully we followed him up the cold, dank and narrow staircase with a musty smell of spider webs and the croaking of lost frogs. The staircase wound up and curled inward inside that massive statue until one was behind the face of the rock-carved figure. From his eyes, which were big as portholes, my grandfather encouraged us to sit and, with our legs swinging over the gargantuan eyelids, we could see far off across the green landscape of meticulous gardens and orchards, and also down, if we dared and did not suffer too badly from vertigo, into the reflection of the lily pond far below us, the lily pads looking tiny from that great height.

The design of the original villa was overseen by Francesco I de' Medici, the Grand Duke of Tuscany in 1581 and he suppos-edly built it to impress his mistress. By the eighteenth century the estate was deserted. Grand Duke Ferdinand III was born in Florence in 1769 and throughout his life he engaged in a multitude of marriages to ladies of high rank and would be bestowed with a great many spectacular titles. They ranged from prince-elector of the Holy Roman Empire to Duke of Salzburg and other impressive names that were taken away as fast as they were given due to the shifting histories of the day. Yet despite a flourish of titles and jobs running principalities and realms, he was born and he would die, in 1824, as the Grand Duke of Tuscany. When he bought the Villa Reale, on the site of what would later be the Villa Demidoff, he decided to demolish the existing villa with the help of explosives. For some unknown reason the debris from this explosive detonation was never cleared away, which would prove, more than a century later, a tremendous boon to my cousin Dimitri and me.

This Habsburg-Lorraine Grand Duke Ferdinand III of Tuscany redesigned the garden before seemingly losing interest in the project. Luckily for us, he left intact a large building near the front gates of the enormous park known simply as the Paggeria, or 'pages' lodging' – part of the former Villa Reale. In 1872 this deteriorating and unkempt compound was sold to Prince Pavel Demidoff, who restored the Paggeria and transformed it into the extremely comfortable Villa Demidoff di Pratolino.

Family members only ever referred to the Villa Demidoff di Pratolino informally as 'Pratolino' despite the extravagant pomp of the uniformed servants lined up awaiting one's arrival or departure. This was a sight which was perfectly normal and something I would never encounter again. The villa was also the scene of wild play where we, the grandchildren, tore around playing with everything, dragging one another in tiny carts and hiding in the autumn hay bales patiently restored by labourers. We played in the endless gardens and near the vast *Appennino*. To us this was merely a playground, though later in life I would learn it was a famous work of art memorialized in etchings and paintings, and sadly known as the *Appennine* – which to my ear is sheer butchery. But that was all still many years off.

At that time, when I was not yet ten years old, everything was a game and there was a lot of laughter and gaiety. They were perhaps the best days of our childhoods. We were extremely fortunate to experience such a luxurious fantasy. In the long hallways where we played with the servants' trolleys, one child lay on the top level, and another child pushed it with all his or her might, letting go near the end of the corridor so that it would smash dramatically into a wall. This was enormous fun. Walls were hung with tapestries and the upstairs corridors, off which were bedrooms, were lined with deep, wide wooden coffers and treasure chests. If we could find the strength to lift the heavy lids there were troves of swords and other booty inside, upon which we would feast our eyes and our imaginations.

One particular room, known simply as the Big Room, was a sitting room the size of a ballroom where my grandfather would play his grand piano. He was a talented musician. Music, for those it speaks to, can save your sanity. My cousin Dimitri remembers our grandfather expertly playing the soulful music of Chopin. As I write these chapters, I am listening to his nocturnes, replaying and lingering on the eighth, and I wonder if this is a sensual time travel taking me back to a place where I knew only joy and cosiness. To us children this room was a favourite vast space where I remember we made forts from pillows taken from sofas the size of boats. In that great room we played for many hours, mixing everything up into make believe – encouraged to do so. Little did we know how accurate this notion of make believe would be, how those halcyon days were fleeting and would never be repeated in our grown-up lives. But it was not for us to know such things then. There was plenty of time still for the undoing of these fairy tales of childhood. At least we had a childhood, unlike my dear grandfather who had none.

These Italian summer holidays always included trips to the gelato shop in the local town – a huge treat. Just as exciting, I remember frequently climbing the fruit trees in the orchards of our garden and sitting astride the limbs of fig trees and feasting on the bursting ripe fruit. Equally thrilling were the elixirs delivered in crystal pitchers, poured into crystal goblets. It was some sort of dark berry concoction – a luscious juice we lapped up on hot afternoons – delivered on silver trays from those kitchens we never so much as considered entering; another world, coexisting and yet entirely separate. This juice was a luxurious treat to us. For all I know it might as easily have been from a store-bought bottle but to us it was manna from heaven and when I think of it my tastebuds awaken and transport me to those sunny, tranquil, carefree times; that sense of elegance I would never know again. But I took it all for granted, as one should as a child; perhaps the only way to appreciate something is to be fully immersed in it and later, with hindsight, and a touch of rue, to look back and be thankful for the unsullied experience.

· From the balcony outside my grandmother's bedroom my cousins and I would watch labourers roll the autumn hay into bales which we would later play on and hide in. From this balcony there was also a clear view of the tops of the ruins of the old Villa Reale. My cousin Dimitri and I passed hours traipsing through that wreckage, Dimitri picking out pieces of mosaic and majolica; me alongside dawdling and daydreaming. In retrospect it is no surprise he would grow up to design jewellery and I would turn to writing, our natural inclinations quietly and naturally flourishing.

In the villa's Big Room, huge doors opened on to sweeping stone steps leading to one of many ornate gardens with genteel, elaborate lawns and well-tended trees. At the back of the Big Room was a concealed doorway you wouldn't know was there. It led to a circular staircase burrowing up and into the private quarters of the villa. I loved that secret passage. For my cousins and me, lucky enough to enjoy some of our childhood in this most glorious playground, these are very fond memories. It was, after all, a time before we knew too much.

The Big Room also housed a sofa that we called 'the boat' and here my grandmother would gather her grandchildren around her and encourage us to make believe we were sailing in a great ship. She would read stories from books to us, fully engaging us and inspiring us. We all worshipped her. She was our own Mary Poppins and we were devoted to her.

My grandfather went out of his way to entertain his grandchildren. He was a warm person with a formal exterior. Life at his Italian villa was governed by protocol. His formal side was something I took for granted and did not question. That I had to kiss his hand and curtsy when I said good morning or goodnight to each of my grandparents did not seem strange to me. My grandparents' life included footmen and chauffeurs and unseen silent maids, and it all seemed perfectly natural to me. Life with my grandparents was a balance between the pinnacles of formality – with curtseying and addressing people by their titles – and relaxed frolicking and afternoon gambols where my grandfather would regale his flock of grandchildren with stories designed to make us laugh or shriek, but always intended to entertain. No one did that for him when he was a child. He never imposed upon us the sadness of his own youth; instead he made sure we enjoyed our time with him. Where did he learn such generosity, I wonder?

Meals, by contrast to the frolicsome play, were exquisitely formal with butlers and uniformed servants emanating from vast kitchens – a part of the house we were not familiar with and yet we knew therein toiled a veritable army. These servants, only ever seen in proper uniforms of greys and whites with hands hidden by gloves, served us at a table covered with the finest of everything from silverware and gold-edged china, again all taken entirely for granted – certainly by me. They were summoned by pressing a Fabergé enamel electric bell which sat on the table in front of my grandmother and she would permit each of us in turn to press it. This was considered by us to be a veritable largesse, and of course we always pressed the little bell far longer than we were supposed to, but that was as far as any misbehaviour went. There were absolutely zero displays of bad manners; it would have been unthinkable. At each meal the grandchildren were seated beside our grandparents in a rotation, so that we looked forward to our turn next to them.

All of us grandchildren were deeply respectful toward our grandparents and it would never have crossed our minds to behave in any other way. This attitude was our pleasure as it conveyed our sentiments of love and appreciation of them and was in no way a tiresome burden or an inconvenient necessity. Quite the opposite. You could say it was all we knew, but on a deep level we did not defy it nor rebel against it. Nor did we see it as an imposition, but rather as a luxury. We knew that much, from our hearts. They treated us with a loving authority. To be told to be respectful by someone acting any other way would of course develop traits of resentment, maybe even rage and a desire for revenge. We experienced no such thing. We adored them and thrived in their company. We were always extremely polite. It would not have occurred to any of us, or even appealed to us, to behave differently.

Sundays at church we were at our most well-behaved in the white marble hexagonal chapel attached to the villa. Here we prayed to the saints and my grandfather played hymns on the organ. It was in this chapel, when I was a baby, that I was baptized by a Russian Orthodox priest. Half the family was Orthodox, the other half Catholic, but these differences meant little to us.

My grandfather was someone I only ever saw impeccably dressed and perfectly behaved; he was the first to inspire a laugh. My time with him, when I was a child, was of long, delicious, hot summers in worlds of impeccable beauty. As I delve into my grandfather's story I see how little I knew then, and yet we were all profoundly and positively affected by his poise and elegant restraint – his very presence – and I hope my words here can be a prayer to him.

~

As I consider Serbia in the late nineteenth century from the perspective of the tree-covered hilltops of Eastern Europe I see smoky medieval farmlands contrasted with earnest city poets. There were 2,000 years of influence from the East and the West. Some people dressed in pantaloons and shoes made of felt and wore fezzes, while others wore long frock coats and pristine white shirts with ties and top hats. Mules dragged carts, dogs ran across unpaved roads and women in smocked long dresses carried tubs of water on the tops of their heads, while others – the rich – drove motorcars with headlamps and glass windows. These stark contrasts launched inevitable foment. The clashing of eras could only spell trouble.

The Balkans are home to a confluence of ancient tribes so old no one knows for sure when they settled or even whence they came. Some say Persia, but no one knows for sure. 'Balkan' itself is a Turkish word meaning 'area of forests'. Serbia's neighbours are rich in legends, such as those of bogeymen and werewolves, Dracula and Vlad the Impaler. Such was Mary Shelley's distillation of the enigmas of this portion of the world that she stoked Bram Stoker's ferocious imagination. *War and Peace* and *Crime and Punishment* were already printed and in the bookstores. The writing, as they say, was on the wall, in festoons of blood. My grandfather's life spanned epochs and crossed borders from a time long gone to a new here and now. Everyone on this new world stage was making up their lines as they went along. Hollywood would say it was great material. Whatever it was, you might not want to live there, breaking bread with vampires.

1893–1903

PRINCE PAUL OF SERBIA WAS THE ONLY CHILD OF PRINCE ARSEN OF SERBIA AND PRINCESS AND COUNTESS AURORA DEMIDOFF DI SAN DONATO.

Imagine, if you will, you are in upscale St Petersburg and it is 1895. You are a plump, healthy toddler of some dozen or so months old and your best friend is your nanny. There is no father, but you do not yet understand the significance of this. Your mother, whom you idolize as if she were a movie star, makes fleeting appearances, but again, you do not yet know any better. Then, one day, without explanation, you are directed to board a train along with a suitcase and your faithful nanny. You are given the responsibility of a heavy, sturdy box made of leather which you must haul about. Your nanny is with you and as of yet you are not the least aggrieved; puzzled, perhaps, but not frightened. After all, why should you be?

Nights and days pass and perhaps gradually you become somewhat disoriented because you have witnessed countless changing landscapes and cityscapes and you have heard languages entirely new to your ear. All this might be rather exciting, even stimulating and interesting, but nothing is explained to you, and obediently you play along with all this inexplicable novelty. Living on a train is quite peculiar. Your nanny, with whom of course you converse in your native Russian, reassures you not to worry; everything is going according to plan. You believe her, of course – why would you doubt her? Days later you reach the home of an older gentleman who is introduced to you as your Uncle Peter, whom you will address as 'Sir'.

You rarely see this man except for Sundays in church and very formal occasions when you are instructed on how to conduct yourself. In any case, he does not pay you too much attention. Three cousins, older than yourself, come and go. They are mostly gone, and in any case not interested in you. You are too young. These cousins are sent to St Petersburg, your previous hometown! They are sent there to school. Perhaps you hear them remonstrate from the safety of the nursery. Inside you wish it was you who was being sent away, home to Russia, except there is no one there any more. Your father has gone back to war, your mother gone who knows where. All you have to remind you of a time before nothing made any sense is your nanny. And with your nanny you converse in your native Russian, but with these new cousins you learn to communicate in French. Your childhood – that time of certainty and safety – is already over.

As this slowly becomes apparent, perhaps you are influenced when you discover your cousins are being sent away to schools in St Petersburg. Perhaps you devise this as a ticket out, a ticket home. Perhaps you petition to be sent away to school. No record reveals why this happened, but your Uncle Peter fires your nanny, sends her back to Russia – never to be seen again – and packs you off to a boarding school in Switzerland; a prison within a prison. French is the language spoken at school and you try to keep up with studies, to fit in and not complain. And you try not to think too much about your nurse who loved you and whom you trusted, but she is gone and she is the one to have delivered you here and then abandoned you. You hate this new life, this boarding school filled with strangers who dismiss you as a foreigner, an outsider. But this indignity is nothing really, merely day terrors, because by night you have another menace with which to contend.

All through those dark night hours, in the freezing school through the Alpine winters, you lie awake no longer able to sleep as you wait for the attacks to begin. Your first few nights you have no idea what awakened you with terrifying and alarming suddenness. Attacked, you sit up, shaking off dreams to see fast moving hairy bulks with long claws bounding across your body, brushing your face. You clear your eyes to see giant rats running across you and your bedclothes with their bright white cleaver teeth, dragging those long rubbery tails. Hell.

When Paul was a year old – and one can only be grateful that he was too young to comprehend the scale of betrayal thrust upon him – his father was already gone. To war, to a mistress, to fight another duel, anywhere – and he had no intention of returning. Paul's mother was equally useless and selfish as far as being a parent goes. The marital union was long since dissolved. Arsen would blame his wife, claiming she ran around on him. Aurora would accuse her husband of being impossible, a tyrant. They were probably both right, to some degree. They were unsuited, that much we can deduce.

Paul's mother had energy enough only to look for another home for her son. She too, emotionally, was already long gone to another clutch of children and had fallen in and out of love with other married men. She was still young, she was beautiful and she was fantastically wealthy. The world around her was morphing from the medieval to modern times, all of which seems to have been lost on her.

Social change was going on all around her. Russian Jews were virtually traipsing past her front door, heading for the relative safety of the new world of the United States of America, as well as a family called Oxenberg that made the journey from the rural lands of Moldova to the brand new city of New York. The story of these Oxenbergs had no bearing whatsoever on the precious existence of Aurora who only looked inward and catered to the desires and foibles of her unhappy heart. It appears her greatest wish was to rid herself of the responsibility of her baby boy. She first asked her older half-brother Elim Demidoff to take the child, but he declined.

Aurora asked around before beseeching her brother-in-law Peter Karageorgević, the exiled king-in-waiting, then living in Geneva. He agreed to take in his nephew and Paul, barely two years old, along with his Russian nurse, was packed off with a one-way ticket to Switzerland. Peter was a man who believed in duty, so while he agreed to lodge his nephew, he acted indifferently toward the little boy. Peter had never emotionally recovered from the death of his beloved wife Zorka and possibly young Paul reminded him of his son Andrew, who had died with her in childbirth and would have been about the same age. Perhaps Paul asked to be sent to boarding school, where his cousins were. Maybe he hoped it was the road home to St Petersburg, except things did not work out that way. Little did he know, for the rest of his strange, appallingly manhandled life, Paul would never again return to Russia.

Around the age of seven, Paul was taken out of school for a very special occasion. I wonder how, or even if, anything was explained to him at the time. I do not know how he reconciled it, but what I do know is that he never forgot the experience because for the rest of his life he talked of this occasion. He was dressed smartly and taken to a train station where he was told to wait patiently. Eventually a train dragged into the station and screeched noisily to a stop. A well-turned-out lady descended from a carriage. She introduced herself to Paul as his mother and then she clutched the confused lad to her. Holding him tight, she told him she loved him. Then she released him. There were tears in her large, tragic, dark eyes. Paul must have been entirely bewildered and unsure what to do or say. Probably he did and said very little. Then the lady turned her back to him, boarded the train and slowly it pulled away from the station. That was it – he was taken back to the boarding school, returned to his lonely life with the rats. There was to be one additional occasion similar to the train station visit, though this time it was a boat and a hug at a dock. Again, this lady told him she was his mother and hugged him. While he remembered these two peculiar interactions, he certainly did not know her. Other than these episodes Paul never saw his mother. That was his entire experience with her. How he grew up to be the loving, caring human being he was defies logic.

When Paul was eleven years old his mother died in Turin and it is unlikely he attended her funeral. For one thing he was a small child and for another he was by now living in Serbia, the reclaimed fatherland. His strange life had already fallen down the next spiral of rabbit holes. Any sort of gentle beginning was by now a very distant memory, if it was a memory at all. And if he was told about his mother's demise I can only speculate what it might have meant to him. I wonder how a young child would process such information. Her life was devoted entirely inward, to her loves and her losses and the concerns of her heart, and she felt not a jot of responsibility toward anyone but herself. Had anyone managed to penetrate her self-centred void and the damage she scattered in her wide wake, one can hope the news would have surprised her. But most likely it would have had little more effect than to have her running to the mirror to see how she looked.

~

In 1903 Uncle Peter was crowned King of Serbia and most of the Karageorgević family, gathering from all over Europe, moved to the 'palace' at Belgrade. This palace was really an army barracks, an all-male court with a strict military way of life. Footage exists of the day of his coronation; he parades down thronged Belgrade boulevards on a white horse dressed in gold and plumes and, after he exits the cathedral, he sports a huge crown which he wears with pride and confidence.

Just one more item on the list of things to transport was his little nephew Paul, the young Prince of Serbia, brought to a country he had never known and to which he was then relocating permanently. The spirit all around him was one of almost celestial triumph. He could not have understood very much, if anything, about Serbia, he did not speak the language, and his introduction was amid an insane backdrop of butchery over which there was undoubtedly rejoicing. Welcome home and try not to step in the coagulating blood.

Welcome home, indeed! He must have wondered where he was truly from and what 'home' could possibly mean. He was born in Russia where he was told he was Serbian, but was now in Serbia and fluent in Russian and French. Never quite fitting in, never fully invited in. Did he worry he had fallen through a wormhole?

A photograph from 1904 of my grandfather newly relocated to the fatherland shows him wearing some sort of antique Serbian ceremonial war attire, albeit from a long-distant era of baggy pantaloons. He is also wearing a fez and posing with two firearms, one of which he hovers over with one hand, as if he is trying not to touch the metal at all, recoiling as his own sensibilities must have recoiled in disgust and terror. He was barely eleven and asked to be a soldier, to give his life for some noble theory. In the photograph he looks traumatized.

In his first decade on Earth he had been propelled from an exquisite mansion in St Petersburg, with his personal nanny, to being an orphan child soldier in the land next door to Dracula, gifted his own set of ornate pistols. He would spend the rest of his days trying to restore his life to a time of civility. Such was the early childhood of my grandfather Paul; emotionally neglected and abandoned on a fundamental level, yet also trained with militaristic discipline and codes of honour. He learned, outwardly at least, to keep his secrets hidden and his face serene, giving away nothing of the dread inside. You would never know it unless, of course, you knew him, as I did. I see his face in that photograph and it is not one of a carefree child.

Paul was given a small room at the top of the palace and this would be his home for the next ten years. This palace was less a place of genteel elegance and more an army fortress. Life there was strict and serious, and the inhabitants all male. It was a forbidding environment, quite the opposite of the happy comforts I would enjoy as a child at our fabled Pratolino. My grandfather's early years saw none of that. Until, that is, he travelled abroad and stayed with relatives. His mind must have been very happily blown open at the thought of what this could mean for him one day. But before that bright path of freedom opened up to him, he lived a deadly serious existence, dressed at all times in his service uniform and schooled and drilled like the soldier he was expected to become. Everyone around him was also in full military dress and ready for battle. Paul was a dutiful and studious boy. He easily mastered many languages and was a diligent student who caused no trouble, except for once when it was discovered he had collected objects that caught his fancy and made for himself a tiny museum display in his cold attic room. It was an early sign of the art collector he would in fact become. But in place of receiving praise for his creative mind he was instead punished for this behaviour, forcing any development of independence inwards. He learned very young how to keep secrets. But he did continue to develop these private inner resources to fulfil some innate need for refinement. He found joy and inspiration in beauty and he looked for it. A weaker person would have given up these pursuits but instead he just kept them to himself.

He filled his free time writing poems and asking after the provenance of beautiful objects he found around the palace. Mostly he made friends among the foreigners who visited his uncle's court, perhaps because he, too, felt he was a foreigner, perhaps to hone his language skills. The top rung, given the times, was made up of the British delegates.

The sentiment of the time was that Britannia ruled the waves, and since initially Britain vociferously did not condone the manner of the restoration of the House of Karageorgević, considering it a savage and illegal coup, the Brits not only refused to acknowledge its credibility, they recalled their representatives. It was their voice on the world stage, backed by the use of newspapers proliferating their opprobrium, their propaganda merely the loudest voice in the room; it ruled the day and influenced public sentiment.

The Brits became all the more important in terms of winning back a position of strength as they had sway over critical issues like sanctions and trade, and therefore food on the table and money in the pockets of peasants dependant on commerce. My grandfather, who was very young, would have been influenced by such sentiments and it would have been natural for him to look to the British for approval, if only because that was what he saw everyone else doing. Everyone else seemed to care very much what the Brits thought, so how could he have seen things any other way? And yet this mirage, this conviction that they were the only civilized people on Earth, was merely a product of the times and heartily encouraged by the Brits themselves, who no doubt believed the hype as much as those they attempted to subordinate. The British appointed themselves the gold standard, and while this worked perfectly in India where a class system was already firmly in place, Serbia was a different beast altogether.

My grandfather, however, was nothing if not neglected and he aspired to be appreciated. It is entirely understandable to me that he should believe these Brits were people to look up to, to admire. This error in judgement would one day cost him everything. But he was just a lonely child at the turn of the century and he made friends with all the foreign diplomats sent to Belgrade, including the Brits, seeking from them the approval he desperately needed. These British delegates opened his eyes to another world – the United Kingdom and its purported civilized style of living. It seemed a far-away place where he would be safe from endless threats of warfare. No doubt this exposure to the Brits helped nurture the idea to attend Oxford University.

Whereas once his greatest worry was attack from rats, now he was faced with having to consider the implications of war. From a young age Paul was influenced by world politics and he made his plans accordingly. Politically, Russia was already lost and deep in turmoil, and in any case, his own parents were no longer there so he had little reason to wish to return. Switzerland had only been a stopping-off place, a stop on the train if you like, along with the hated boarding school, so hardly a place to hanker for. Now Serbia was facing worldwide public opprobrium followed by two Balkan wars. No doubt Paul saw Britain as a bridge to safety. He was dutiful but he was never a warrior and had no desire at all for warfare. He did not even like to play with his cousin George, famously entranced with guns to the extent that one day by accident he shot to death a manservant. Paul, instead, preferred classical music and master paintings.

Because his health was considered frail, a teenage Paul was frequently sent for summer holidays to spas in Western Europe. These trips brought him into contact with his Demidoff and Abamelek-Lazarev family connections, his direct and personal links to the ruling King and Queen of Italy. Paul was welcome here and he was grateful on many levels. He was quick to recognize what he liked, and he liked refinement. He was, himself, a gentleman, in the truest sense of the meaning, and to the end of his days he would remain steadfastly so.

Bucking the tradition of Karageorgević men being educated in prestigious military schools in France or Russia, Paul requested he be sent to England to complete his studies, specifically to Oxford University. One of the many benefits to these overland journeys to England meant evermore opportunities to stop in at the comfortable villas of relatives. Each time he left Serbia he went directly to stay with his favourite aunt, Moina (Maria), and he refuelled his sensibilities on opulence. Was it from his great-uncle Anatole he got the gene, or was it developed from the contrast of life in Serbia, a shocking backwater of medieval squalor and peasantry? Unlike his cousins, Alexander and George, Paul was not tempted by firearms and power plays, but always preferred refinement. This never made him less of a Serb, not in my eyes; merely a different type. There are as many artists in Serbia as there are warriors, but all share a sense of unshakeable patriotic nationalism overriding what might otherwise have been seen as differences. His loyalty was irrefutable, just like a Serb; his belief in truth and in duty were unshakeable, just like a Serb; his respect for the meaning of friendship was unwavering, again, so very Serbian.

Having been endlessly marginalized by the Karageorgević clan, it is easy to see why Paul cleaved to his maternal family line where he was welcomed with open arms and gorgeous trinkets. The decision was an easy one to make. Yet he never walked away from Serbia, not in reality and not in his heart. His plan was to bring what he loved most about the West, in the form of a first-class museum, to his homeland Serbia, where in the strangest possible way, he was treated as something of a foreigner. Identity crises on multiple levels did neither defeat nor deter him. He would buy the finest and the best he could find, and he would open that museum. He made it his life's commitment. In this he did achieve his goal and he should be remembered and appreciated. Today that museum exists, but its doors are locked. One day it will be my great pleasure to see those doors opened.

For their part, these relatives welcomed him, with his Aunt Moina always inviting him to her Villa Demidoff and his 'adopted' aunt, Queen Elena of Italy – who had long nurtured a soft spot for him – having him to stay with her in Rome and also at her luxurious palazzo in Tuscany. He must have been deeply tempted to stay forever. His life was an anachronism, a mix of conflicting epochs.

In 1913 he was accepted to Oxford University. He swiftly updated his wardrobe to fit with a modernizing Britain and set himself up at Christ Church. He must have been beyond jubilant. He loved this new access to camaraderie, to friendships of peers interested in the arts and culture – just as he was – and his feelings for his new crowd were real. He should not have been quite so trusting, but how was he to know? Certainly he enjoyed his British acquaintances but unlike these jolly fellows with their precious padded lives and preoccupations with balls and fancy dress, he always watched from a step back because he was obliged to keep an eye on world politics, especially as they concerned Serbia. What happened to Serbia would invariably impact his life, and he did not know then to what degree.

My grandfather's life was a conundrum of extremes. Almost at once, after this first gust of abundant joy with his new, safe, civilized, intellectual life in England there was the matter at Sarajevo and the assassination of Archduke Franz Ferdinand. Paul's life in England was abruptly interrupted when the Austro-Hungarian Empire declared war on Serbia.

If he knew nothing else, Paul knew he was a member of the realm, of the fighting force, and that his presence, armed and in attendance, was required. He immediately notified the university of his need to leave, and while his British friends fussed over invitations to shooting parties and who got to dally with David (the future King and Duke of Windsor) at balls and polo games,

Paul departed at once for Belgrade to put on his uniform, pick up his rifle and report for duty, whatever that might be.

Paul spent the winter of 1914–15 in Belgrade and it was as if he had journeyed to an alternate universe, consumed as it was with the hideousness that is war. Deaths by typhoid outnumbered warfare losses and the atmosphere, quite generally, was hellish for everyone. In 1915 he made his way to Rome, operating as a trustworthy emissary and he followed this up with an extended excursion to England where he stayed with friends, convalescing. He had no stomach for war but he fulfilled his duty and in 1916 he travelled to Corfu, where his uncle King Peter and the entire Serbian government were set up; a de facto Serbia. King Peter had famously led his troops across Albania to safety aged seventy-one, an act of heroism from which his health would never fully recover. Until the end of the war, Paul stayed with his uncle in Corfu and worked with the Red Cross.

In 1918 – back in Belgrade – Paul's cousin Alexander was, effectively, running Serbia conjointly with his father, King Peter. Paul, now twenty-five, gratefully returned to Oxford to complete his studies and earn his 'war' degree. His upper-class schoolmates were a hive of invitations to parties and other frivolity which must have been an overwhelming relief after his recent life-threatening experience. All the more reason for him to revel in his time spent in England, in the comforts of culture and civilized life. No wonder he loved his English friends. Too bad he never saw their quiet disdain for him, his status as a foreigner proving an insurmountable hurdle in British society. It is interesting that his best friends throughout his life were other foreigners, like Chips Channon, a fantastically wealthy American, and Bernard Berenson, an American Jew and the art connoisseur of the day.

It was during these years he made friends with Lady Elizabeth Bowes-Lyon, and the suggestion of a union was whispered in the wings. Instead, she would become the future Queen Mother. Paul also met men like Winston Churchill, who was by then deep into politics and already taking himself extremely seriously, and also, unfortunately, a Brit named Anthony Eden. Churchill and Eden would never appreciate my grandfather's qualities. And their personal animosity would come back to haunt my grandfather years later, and almost destroy him. He could not have known to what extent this hostile relationship would wreck his life.

I have read the letters Churchill wrote to his mother at a young age during his years at boarding school and they are full of accusations about his younger brother, essentially ratting him out at every turn and at the same time begging his mother to send him money for more snacks. Such was his personality as a young child. It explains a lot. He had a childish mind that, given the treatment he imposed upon my grandfather in later years, he never grew out of. I can never forgive him for this, and while indisputably he did great things for England, he is no hero in my eyes. He is a double-dealing liar and a smarmy coward. I never saw him at the front line on a battlefield. He stayed home, chomping on his cigars, overeating, and spouting pithy quotes. If you need proof to support my opinion please see the internal memos sent between Eden and Churchill during the war years, where they refer to my grandfather by a derisive nickname they coined for him. Childish, but also unforgivable. They destroyed his life, or tried to; or rather, they did not care if they did.

However, long before all this, a genial, more naive Paul finished up his studies at Oxford and elected to stay on in England, enjoying his friends and this fun new life. He misread these relationships and that would prove nearly fatal. It did not help that his cousin Alexander kept him at arm's length, politically. But Paul had his inheritance, so as there was no official position offered him in Serbia he invented a life for himself. He was perfectly content to accept all further exposure to his Italian and Russian relatives and their appealing lifestyles at homes like the Villa Demidoff and the Villa Abamelek in Rome. They were more or less museums – marble splendours filled with the absolute best of the best. All this had developed his eye. Apart from socializing, he began to fill his time with collecting paintings and gradually, always thinking of Serbia as home, despite the vagueness that might imply, he began to make plans to open an art museum in Belgrade. He would bring what he loved to this country he was part of, no matter how ill-defined his bond.

By 1922 his cousin, now King Alexander, was planning the Tomb of the Unknown Soldier at Avala, the hilltop overlooking Belgrade from the south. Paul, already a recognized art specialist and excellent marriage candidate, began looking for a wife. He was artistic, he was a piano player, and he had a sense of humour, but he was no sissy and he never complained. He was uniquely resilient and I believe this was his Serbian side. He was, after all, a Serb.

HRH Princess Olga of Greece and Denmark

11 June 1903 – 16 October 1997

ON THE AFTERNOON OF 18 MARCH 1913, KING GEORGE embarked on his daily stroll without the presence of his body-guards. He had been warned not to go out unaccompanied on the streets of the newly-liberated city of Thessaloniki, but he would not be deterred. While the King was passing a cafe, a man later identified as Alexandros Schinas shot him in the back. The sixty-seven-year-old monarch collapsed and died almost instantly. A messenger ran and informed the King's third-eldest son, Prince Nicholas, of the news. Nicholas was then tasked with telling his elder brother Constantine that he was now King.

The tradition of Europe's royals was based on generations of marriages between Russian tsars and Prussian princesses, Habsburg archdukes and Romanov imperial grand duchesses, English kings and Spanish infantas, French dauphins and Austrian archduchesses. If you're into titles let's not forget that Marie Antoinette's father was a Holy Roman Emperor. Queen Victoria, a German who knew exactly what she was doing, ably assigned her bountiful progeny to the most opulent royal houses available. These unions were a means of binding Europe's otherwise tribal and warlike factions. Machiavelli explains it all very clearly. Royalty was always first and foremost, behind the pomp, a political device to create protection against the menace of those who would try and take it away.

The Greek royal family – in reality a branch of the House of Glücksburg – was installed as a fait accompli in 1863 as a means of including this tantalizing outpost under the auspices of the great armies of Europe; a precursor to NATO, if you like.

Speaking very generally, royalty was more a matter of strategy than micro-management governance, though there are plenty of exceptions. The point, however, was to strengthen the militarily or geopolitically weak. Thus, King Christian IX of Denmark and Princess Louise of Hesse-Kassel's second son Vilhelm, who had never set foot in the land of Greece, would, by consensus of the 'Powers', be crowned under a new name as George I King of the Hellenes. Greece, with its tantalizing ports and seafaring trade routes was under threat of siege since the first days of international trading; in other words, millennia. It was simply too practical a property to ignore, rendering it endlessly vulnerable and repeatedly besieged.

These elaborate schemes worked well in the main, but could not be fully relied upon. In 1913 King George I was assassinated. This act of aggression did not so easily rid the Greeks of their foreign overlords. At most it only succeeded in a reorganization; the dead king was immediately succeeded by his son Constantine, Duke of Sparta. King Constantine, whether the Greeks wanted him or not, enjoyed the full support of all the crowned heads of Europe and their formidable armies. Besides, there were more where Constantine came from, as he had four brothers and two sisters, all of whom at this point saw themselves as natives, having been born in Greece. They did not consider themselves foreigners. Constantine's third brother, Prince Nicholas of Greece, was the father of my grandmother HRH Princess Olga of Greece and Denmark – Amama to me.

THE PRINCESS MYTH

The first ten years of Princess Olga's life were perfection itself. She lived the dream which young girls all over the world envisage when they gush – usually dressed in graceful gowns on their wedding day – 'I feel like a princess!' Feeling like a princess, or being 'treated like royalty' (another much-overused and misunderstood expression) is nothing like the real thing. And just as well! In short, this is because when you are royalty you live with the possibility that everything you thought was yours can be stripped away, down to your very bed. The divide between the romantic concept of royalty and the reality of the position is as wide as the universe. Long live the dreamers, I say, but beware what you wish for. I ask you this simple question: do you think you could cope if after being granted your airy, vague dream it was all rent asunder, your family members decapitated, your own homeland disavowing you, changing you into some sort of carnival freak show refugee? Because that is what happens to real princesses. Not all of them, to be sure, but look at the Romanovs, look at Louis XVI and his lovely Marie Antoinette, look around a little closer and ask yourself again just exactly what it is about being a princess you crave. The clothes?

Prince Nicholas of Greece was not the type to run off and live the life of a bohemian artist, even though he was a capable artist and talented writer. Nicholas lived by the codes of tradition and duty: on 29 August 1902 he married Her Imperial Highness Grand Duchess Elena Vladimirovna Romanova of Russia who became, upon her marriage, Her Imperial and Royal Highness Princess Eleni of Greece and Denmark. Elena was the granddaughter of Tsar Alexander II of Russia, and the daughter of Grand Duke Vladimir Alexandrovich of Russia. Elena and Nicholas would have three daughters: Olga, born 11 June 1903; Elizabeth, born 24 May 1904; and Marina, born 13 December 1906.

My grandmother, Princess Olga, was born in the royal Tatoi Palace in Athens, a princess of Greece and Denmark at a time when her grandfather was the ruling king of the land. Her mother was a close relative of the imperial Romanov tsar. Olga's lineage was impeccable and if she thought about her future at all it would have been free of doubts or any sort of worry. Instead, her head was full of images of princes to marry and palaces in which to reside. Such was all she knew. As a happy, well-tended child she was soon joined by two sisters, and all three would be best friends for the rest of their days. This tight bond would never break, regardless of the upheavals of their lives. Perhaps this tightness was in part due to the shocking uncertainties the hand of fate dealt them.

These sisters would grow up to be tall and slender and exotically lovely, becoming known internationally as the most beautiful women of their time. But before they reached this heady height there would be some unexpectedly treacherous obstacles to clear. Their first decade on Earth was blissful, a real live fairy tale. One perfect decade, and then it was over.

In 1913, when my grandmother Olga was ten years old, she learned that her grandfather George, the King of Greece, had been assassinated. Her uncle Constantine was installed as King but by 1914 the world as they knew it was over. The previously unthinkable freight train of incalculable bad news was bearing down on all of them, carriages loaded with the bayonets of discontented populations, shuttling fast into view. The dream days were over.

In 1914 World War I started and Russian Bolsheviks whipped up the incontrovertible grievances of the times. Russia was on fire. The lives of Olga's mother's family were quite specifically in the sight lines and the killings were personal. Children are not usually aware of foreign wars, but in this case, family members were hunted and murdered and she would have known of it all. By 1917, Olga's relatives – the Romanov grand dukes – were chased across the Caucasus, tracked down and shot to death, killed for sport like trophies. In 1918 the tsar and his immediate family members were gathered in a basement and executed. Olga was barely fifteen years old.

So I ask all you young ladies clamouring for princess status and admiring yourselves in mirrors in your prom gowns and your store-bought tiaras, do you know what you mean when you say you 'feel like a princess'? Are you strong enough, durable enough, resilient enough to survive the bad times? Or would you run right home to your suburban enclaves of gated communities and cul-de-sacs and mall shopping? How would you deal with your freedoms removed and your lives at threat? For now, your greatest concern is which handsome football star will escort you to the dance where you will likely binge drink and throw up on your lace gown while your escort gallantly holds back your pretty tresses. None of that touches the life of a real princess (except those from Monaco, but that's another story). Not in the real world. Sorry to burst your bubble, but someone had to do it so it may as well be me.

In 1917 King Constantine was forced to abdicate and his son Alexander became king, but in name only. The rest of the Greek royal family, fearing for their lives, made Switzerland their base and prepared to wait and watch – living in political exile, unceremoniously evicted from their homeland of Greece and despatched into the void. From a once otherworldly life in a palace, the family was now scurrying around Europe searching for affordable lodging. Overnight they had no country, no home, no means, few prospects, and growing insecurity. Shockingly, they found out they were poor.

No one was prepared for this eventuality, but interestingly – and this is the backbone of my argument of the difference between the real thing and the imagined lifestyle – these royals managed. They coped and they adjusted. The myth of the princess completely overlooks the dark side, the great demands that might cripple a weaker-minded person. The myth ignores the life-threatening consequences. Is that really what all those young girls dream of – do they have any idea what it all means? I believe they see only party frocks and shiny tiaras and they ignore the dangers.

I knew of my grandmother's life because she openly spoke about it. She even mentioned wearing tiaras and how uncomfortable and heavy they were, and what a worry it was that they should not fall off! But also I saw her life replayed in hundreds of black-and-white photographs she had carefully preserved in slim, elegant albums. I saw pictures of palaces and people wearing magnificent costumes, lots of long dresses, starched military uniforms, medals, sashes and jewellery so enormous and magnificent as to overshadow anything you will see in today's world.

I was never much clued-up on the difficulties and troubles of her life, not because she did not mention them, but rather because of the manner in which she spoke of these events, always lightly, always matter-of-factly. She told us stories of glory and times of woe, but she never shed a tear of self-pity. These grandparents of mine were from another time, when people knew how to conduct themselves, if only in public. As you will see from the personal diaries of my grandmother, her inner thoughts were at odds with her external behaviour. She suffered, she worried, she wrestled consciously with depression, but she never let on – she never complained.

What a difference from the modern indulgence of the cult of victimhood. It is not that people today are weaker, it is merely their training to let it all hang out, but my vote goes to the ways of my grandparents where they kept their greatest doubts to themselves, and that was their coping mechanism. Given what they dealt with I can only admire them all the more. Now that I think about it, while my grandmother frequently spoke about some of the darkest days of her youth, she never presented herself as self-absorbed or tragic. Quite the contrary, she kept it real, but she kept it light. I remember her sweet face with her dark green eyes and her easy, shy smile. She was only comfortable in the presence of close family members. It was one of my greatest blessings to spend time with her and bask in her elegant and cosy company.

When I was in my twenties I often visited my grandmother at her house in Paris and I thought I knew her well. She was always meticulous and organized, and perfectly and simply put together: quiet silks and pearls and low-heeled shoes. For jewels she preferred enormous pearls and fat emeralds, and those were just for everyday wear. I loved her dearly and I knew her as a gentle soul, someone I felt happy to be with whose company I appreciated. Daily, she filled crossword puzzles and played solitaire on a green felt card table, and she kept a box of caramels on a low shelf although she was always extremely disciplined and never had more than a few per day. It was one of those tiny treats she permitted herself, always moderate, always in control. In the house on the rue Scheffer, in the smaller intimate sitting room used only for close family, I would listen to her on the telephone, an old-style bulky black rotary machine, and I would hear her chatting in any one of the dozens of languages she spoke fluently. It was perfectly customary to my ear to hear this multiplicity of languages, except for Serbian (Serbo-Croatian, as it was known in those days), which no doubt my grandmother spoke fluently, but I never heard a word of it spoken by any family member.

At the time I did not even know to question this. There were the homes and towns and names of loyal generals and disloyal politicians, and all of them were only ever introduced in their original Slavonic, in such a familiar way. None of us ever stumbled over the pronunciations, as no doubt a British diplomat would! It was perfectly natural to us; so natural we didn't even acknowledge it happening. It would never have occurred to any of us to Anglicize these names and I grew up perfectly pronouncing names like Bled, Brdo, Vojvodina, even Dedinje, and personal names such as Mihaylović, Simić, Apis, and of course Karageorgević and Obrenović. Even that final ć was nothing strange to me. I pronounced all these like a native – not that I realized that then – but now, as I study the language, I realize in fact it is not so foreign after all. Most glaring to me of these examples is the house we knew as Beli Dvor; it turns out my very first Serbian words were 'White Palace'. This was a house my grandparents lived in during their strange years as a married couple and when my grandfather was installed as regent.

In the troubled years of the late 1930s, Beli Dvor, which I pronounce exactly as a native would, was part of a magnificent royal complex called Dedinje; a marble extravaganza fit for a king, which was precisely its purpose. Beli Dvor was meant to house the three sons of King Alexander: Peter, Tomislav and Andrej. Situated in the park of Dedinje, it is a stately square house with an entranceway of black and white marble and a perfect sweeping staircase. Instead it would be occupied, years after the death of King Alexander, by my still-homeless grandparents for whom no special provision of a residence was made despite the fact my grandfather was now regent. I leave it up to you, dear reader, to interpret the possible meanings of such treatment. I have my own opinions; I think it is best I keep them to myself.

No one in my childhood ever spoke of this building as anything but Beli Dvor, or with anything but regret and love, a place they missed and wished to return to. I knew it almost as a fiction, a holy grail. It is enormously significant that I was permitted to write the last few chapters of this book in the royal palace complex. My view from the gatehouse of the feminine, graceful outlines of this almost mythic house has been impactful. It has in some small sense changed my life and for this I am forever grateful. I think I will never stop my heart from smiling at the blessing of this great good fortune, this closing of the loop, the full circle from those who left unwillingly all the way to me who came here out of curiosity, and got stuck in the mud of love. This has been a mystical part of a long lost past. It was the house in which my mother was born and where she spent the first five years of her life. It was her home. To me, and to all my maternal family it was only ever Beli Dvor. So, without acknowledgement, there was a modicum of Serbian spoken.

Today, with wider eyes and a deeper understanding, I see that there was always a part of us that was indeed raised Serbian, whether we knew it or not. And when I hear people refer to this house as the White Palace, I gasp in horror and am insulted by the paltry need to make it English. Is it too difficult for them to pronounce? I laugh at this, as if I was a native listening to the clumsy efforts of a foreigner. This tiny detail, this little inkling of a link – my first link – warms me, touches me, and reinforces my new vision of myself as a Serb. I was a Serb all along, except I only just found that out. I could not be more proud. I beam.

I grew up surrounded by a multitude of languages and we pronounced names according to their provenance, such as the Villa Pratolino with its statue – the *Appennino* – or the Tour Eiffel, or HRH Princess Maria Pia di Savoia. We pronounced the names of our relatives in the language of their origins, regardless of where they may have been born or where they lived, or even in which country we were when we spoke of them. There were no meaningful borders for us, from nowhere and from everywhere. No names were Anglicized because, for one thing, none of us were British; we were from all over, we were a multilingual con-glomerate and we hailed from everywhere. And while no one lived in their own original homeland, we did not homogenize and distil our heritage, we added to it, making for an extraordinary tribe all our own. Gatherings of family members were occasions where many languages were spoken at the same time. We could all understand one another with perfect ease but an outsider would have had trouble.

My grandmother, for example, skipped easily from Russian to Danish to German to French to English to Italian, and, of course, to her native Greek, and even to a little Swahili from her days in Kenya. These years in Africa she spoke of as if they had been an experience, rather than the tragedy they were. She recounted her years there as merely a simple tale to tell. She never gave the sense that she felt sorry for herself, though she would express her sadness at the evident damage done to her husband and to her children, and in these discourses she always included young King Peter – the child she half reared with her cousin Queen Maria – whom she was forced to leave behind in Serbia after their own expulsion. She never forgot him and she never reconciled her feelings for the inexcusable child abuse inflicted upon him. She had even tried, naively perhaps, to save him, but it backfired and this was a sadness she never got over, even though she never recounted it that way. It was just the way she spoke of him that implied, at least to me, that she felt she had failed him. It pained her.

This was a lady who cared intimately about family and she felt she had not done her part, overlooking the impossibility of it all and how very far beyond her reach it was to have made any kind of difference. It was all out of her hands, politically, but it was something that was never out of her heart. I doubt Peter ever knew that, or if he did whether he could believe it, so brainwashed was he by his handlers, this young abused child king. Another wrecked life, made all the sadder for the loneliness of it, leading to an excruciatingly hideous end. Collateral damage is what the politicians would have glibly ascribed it to. Child abuse – illegal, unscrupulous and unforgivable – is how I see it; but more on that later.

When my grandmother spoke to me of her greatest sadness in her life it was predictably personal: devoid of politics, devoid of the unfair hand fate had dealt her; the full-scale murder of the way of life she was born into. Instead, the only regret she voiced was outliving her sisters; her best friends. And here we touch upon the issue of trust: the only people she ever fully and entirely trusted – and can you blame her after such a life? – were her sisters. Trust, in my opinion, is the single most critical element in human relationships. Once damaged it can never be repaired. Among her sisters there was 100 per cent trust, even though their lives and political sentiments differed throughout those crazy 1930s. I believe this single element was what got them through an otherwise grotesque pile-up of consequences.

In Paris, in the 1970s, I rode buses with my grandmother. When leaving the house she wore a 1950s-style turban on her head and she also wore gloves. She did not like me to tuck my hair behind my ears and I, too, had to wear gloves. The princess learned the routes of the buses and together we would wait at the stop. She would have our fares prepared, working soft, sand-coloured, gloved fingers into a leather coin purse. My grandparents had a house in Paris, with its own garage and even a car and a chauffeur. Over time, after my grandfather died, my grandmother decided she could get around on her own.

That may not sound radical. Consider, however, that this was the same princess who only a few years before had been paraded through a thronged city's streets in an open carriage drawn by six white horses and coachmen in powdered wigs, wearing a heavily bejewelled crown on her head. In the scope of things that was not long ago; yet it was an age.

Olga and her two sisters spoke to one another in their native Greek; with pet names for all their relatives they communicated almost in a code of their own devising. In letters, too, their missives are near impenetrable due to their constant use of nicknames; their private world kept all the more exclusive – out of necessity or habit or fun I cannot say – but it suited them and gave them a sense of privacy in an otherwise untrustworthy world. It was important to my grandmother throughout her life to feel connected to a personal web of close and trusted relatives. I surmise this was a coping mechanism after her life of epic traumas. Family members endured assassinations and exile when Olga was still barely a teenager. Russian cousins had fared badly. Grotesquely. This was not paranoia. None of this is ever included in the fairy tales perpetuated in children's books – and for good reason. Only Hans Christian Andersen alluded to this darker side and children could barely listen without having nightmares.

My grandmother loved and respected both her parents and often spoke of them in adoring terms. She understood what family meant and the importance of the union. My grandmother and I spent many hours looking through her photo albums. There were photos of her as a child with her Romanov relatives in enormous palaces in Russia, gathered in heavy ceremonial costumes with massive jewels and plumes and swords and medals. Everything was very grand and serious. Her own wedding photographs were of white horses and carriages. These worlds she showed me were already long gone. My grandmother would tell me who everyone was and how we were related, patiently and happily poring over the pictures. We did that often and I loved hearing the stories. I don't think I appreciated the significance of what she had been through. I never considered the weight of exile and banishment from homelands, the impossible dread of assassinated family members, the uprooting, the endless upheavals.

Everyone has a story to tell, no one gets through life unscathed. I apologize for shattering any illusions but let me assure you being a princess is no promise of a plush, padded life. It can be, but as with real life, or any type of life, there are no guarantees.

When my grandmother was seventeen years old she had already experienced exile and financial insecurity, as well as the murder of a great many relatives. She had seen her parents plunged into despair over where and how to survive. She saw and endured so much more than she was prepared for. However, she loved her parents and she loved her younger sisters and she firmly believed in family and duty. Together, as a team, they faced their suddenly very uncertain lives and unclear futures. One thing became abundantly clear and that was the necessity of all the girls marrying well. Olga knew it was essentially her duty, and duty was something she fully understood and respected, and never considered remonstrating against. She was a team player.

To add to the sadness of Olga's life her cousin, King Alexander, died a lonely death in Athens in 1920, with none of his family around him. He had been held, trapped; more or less a political prisoner. In December 1920 King Constantine was recalled to Greece by plebiscite, and in the autumn of 1921 Prince Nicholas and his family left Switzerland to return to Tatoi Palace – the family home in Athens. After four years in exile being at home in Athens with virtually every member of the family present was a glorious time. Life was seemingly back to normal. However, the need to make good marriages for Elena and Nicholas's three ravishing daughters – if only to better protect their suddenly questionable futures – was imperative.

In the early spring of 1922 Princess Elena moved to Cannes. She brought with her Olga and Elizabeth who were then aged eighteen and seventeen respectively. As hoped, almost at once Olga's remarkable looks and simplicity of manner caught the attention of Crown Prince Frederik of Denmark, known to his friends as Rico. The possibility of a marriage to Rico was much hoped for and luckily Rico seemed to fall in step with the plan as if on cue. An official engagement followed and he was invited to Athens. His visit was considered a huge success. Olga was now nineteen years old, but not nearly as confident or carefree as she ought to have been. This union was more than just a safe landing for her, it was also a way to relieve her parents' stress. She was well aware of her duty. Her diary, which she began about this time, shows her as a pious teenager conscious of her role as the eldest daughter and longing to think 'the right thoughts' and 'feel the right feelings'.

Paris was a centre for many rootless royals; Princess Elena arrived with Olga, Elizabeth and Marina in the last week of July with the plan that Rico would meet them there. Olga was there, in full view of a large cross-section of her family, waiting. As far as anyone knew the engagement was still on and both had agreed to meet to discuss the future. With Olga spoken for, Princess Elena left for London with Elizabeth and Marina; there were still two more daughters to present.

My grandmother kept a daily diary and what I know about writers is that you only write if you are a writer. Therefore, unacknowledged though it was, she was a writer. So was another of my forebears, the dandy Anatole Demidoff, so from both lines I inherit the writer gene and it is my intention to use this skill to do good as best I can. My grandmother wrote in small booklets, using ink pens of green or blue, in her tidy, slanted handwriting and every day of every year she entered a note. It is from these little books the following material is retrieved. I feel extremely fortunate to have her here, co-authoring this chapter, if you like, in her own words.

The following excerpts, directly from my grandmother's diaries, begin when she was nineteen years old. The first entry is from those mortifying days when she was left alone in Paris, waiting for her betrothed, Rico, Crown Prince Frederik of Denmark, who seemed to have evaporated right in front of her already-disillusioned dark green eyes.

PRINCESS OLGA'S DIARIES

MONDAY, 5 SEPTEMBER 1922

We have been writing and discussing what is best to do as Mummy telegraphed to R. to come on Friday. As we want to be quiet to discuss things and see him privately, Marie-Therese thought this house would be best and quietest as the Ritz would be impossible. I only hope now Mummy will consent to come here at once and leave the others at the Ritz with Nursie and stay here with me quietly till it is all over one way or another… In a few days my life will be decided, I do wish it were over…

Mummy and the girls arrive this evening by the 9.40 train… we have been bombarding Mummy with telegrams begging her to come here alone and that I should stay here to see Rico quietly as meeting at the Ritz would be fatal. Happily the Greek family left last night so there is time to prepare the rooms for Woolly [Elizabeth's nickname] and Marina. Mummy telegraphed yesterday saying she would come here! Marie-Therese telephoned to the Danish legation to check when R. was arriving and they said this evening at 11 and not tomorrow as we thought… If only I knew in what state of mind he is in! Is he still bitter and resolved to break off the engagement? I only hope he will listen to me and after that if he still remains the same it means he never really loved me! God will help me to say the right things!

All is finished now between Rico and me, he came on Friday at three and I saw him first. We remained three quarters [of an hour] talking but he had quite made up his mind to give it up. I said I was willing to try again but he said he had no more love for me (it couldn't have been very strong while it was there). I insisted upon seeing him here quietly to avoid the Ritz. Mummy out of delicacy didn't see him first not to let him think she was trying to influence him, while he without the least decency or tact had already been to the Ritz in the morning to see Christo, and again, just before coming here to see Woolly alone, to ask her how to speak to me and what to say!! Before leaving I gave him back the ring and he also said he was glad we had parted 'without bad words'.

⁓

Olga was twenty and she was distracted with worry for herself and her family, suffering seemingly at the arbitrary hands of fate. Perhaps no 'bad words' were spoken with Rico but rejection for anyone is wounding, and for a young lady whose life was in upheaval this inexplicable dismissal might have been unnerving, to say the least. However, fully overshadowing this blow, King Constantine of Greece was forced to abdicate on 27 September 1922. The crushing defeat of the Greek army at the hands of the Turks in Asia Minor had forced her uncle to leave the country. His son George was handed the crown but the rest of the royal family were required to leave. Constantine and his family left for Corfu and from there they moved to Palermo. Prince Nicholas left Greece with his family. All the while his brother knew full well that the future would involve considerable hardship. For Prince Nicholas's daughters, whose ages ranged from fifteen to nineteen, the outlook was particularly bleak.

SUNDAY, 18 SEPTEMBER

The whole thing is such a tremendous nightmare... They thought that this time it is all finished, that uncle Tino will never rule over the country again and perhaps never see it again... Georgie, King!! And for how long? No one knows if it wouldn't enter their heads to kick him out! Then it will mean a republic and we won't ever see... The place... Again...! Home, the house... Oh! No, God won't let it come to that. However, things are so bad one must be ready for everything. Perhaps God wants to punish us for our lack of faith and principles, thinking we can act without Him.

~

One week after the royal family set sail from Greece, Princess Elena left Paris and joined her husband Nicholas in Palermo. Their immediate concern was to find accommodation for the winter. They were virtually without means of support and their ability to bring their daughters out into society was severely curtailed.

~

MONDAY, 3 OCTOBER

I am here at the Ritz since over a week. Mummy left for Palermo on Thursday morning and must have got there on Saturday night. No telegram has come yet. We are just living 'sur la branche' [on a limb] and one can hardly realize this is the second exile and we are one small tribe like wandering Jews with no home to go to! Oh! It is too awful and I feel so stunned, I refuse to grasp it all! It seems 1 million refugees have arrived in Athens and an order has been issued that every house has to take in two of them and that all empty houses have to be occupied at once!

~

The news from Athens was worse each day. Prince Christopher, who finally arrived safely in Palermo, reported by letter that Prince George was essentially in solitary confinement while Prince Andrew and family were under armed guard. In Palermo the exiles were beginning to get on each other's nerves and Olga's parents were longing to get away, either to San Remo or to Grasse, and find somewhere cheap to rent.

On 22 October the three sisters left for San Remo and Olga realized immediately this quiet town was to be her prison. No one in the family had any idea how long this nightmare was to last. Losing the security of a homeland and a united family, surely Olga realized her chances of meeting anyone appropriate now, when she was at exactly the age for it, were evermore unlikely. And after Rico, she might have doubted herself; probably even blamed herself.

Olga arrived on Thursday, 23 November with her two sisters and their old nanny Miss Fox. Their hotel – 'this godforsaken place' – was perched on a hilltop. Inside, the rooms were 'perfectly foul, plush on all the furniture, heavy wooden beds and few bathrooms. One might as well be in Brindisi.' Terrified that their companion, a Mrs Beaumont (who had rearranged the rooms '*a sa guise*' [to her liking] and who found them delightful) might persuade her mother to like them too, Olga anxiously awaited the arrival of her parents.

On 1 December, the day after Marina's sixteenth birthday, Olga's parents arrived. Prince Nicholas had not seen his daughters for five months and the reunion was thrilling, despite the backdrop of total insecurity. A tiny light of hope flared on 2 December when Olga happily penned: 'P & M don't seem very enchanted with the hotel, happily.'

However, the family had no cash, and the chance of a move either into a larger villa or to another place altogether vanished. Their days consisted of windswept seaside and mountain walks, teas at the English tea room, bridge games with virtual strangers and the ever anxious lookout for the postman. Life was oppressive.

It made even the prospect of a drive in a rickety Fiat and a day's excursion to Cannes seem like the greatest imaginable treat. As winter approached, the weather was reliably rainy and damp, mirroring the family's mood.

Christmas was a subdued occasion. Their presents to one another were 'little handkerchiefs and toy tablecloths bought in Paris the previous month.' Their governess did best of all: she got a pair of 'washing gloves sewn with black.' Their days were all alike apart from infrequent visits from friends.

~

TUESDAY, 19 DECEMBER

Friends arrived for one day having driven over from Nice for the night. They took us to lunch at the Royal where the hotel and food is not to be compared with this. I was so pleased to see [her friend] again.

~

The visitors gave the three girls beautiful presents and admired Olga's little black Scots terrier, Yankee.

~

SATURDAY, 30 DECEMBER

A telegram arrived saying that Uncle Tino was dead. He passed away that morning in Palermo from a stroke.

~

The effect on the family was devastating and that same night Prince Nicholas and Princess Elena took the train for Naples. Over the next few weeks Olga went into a deep depression. She could not stand the thought that her uncle's death, which meant so much to her and her exiled family, could mean so little to the people of Greece. She tried to uplift herself with lofty thoughts but her unhappiness was intense.

~

JANUARY 1923

I can't take my mind away from this awful grief which becomes more acute every day, it is no use, I can't realize it... I feel so crushed, my thoughts are no more of my own; sometimes I feel I am going to burst.

~

Olga felt relief at a proposed move to Florence: 'There are such a lot of beautiful things to see.' But in reality their stay in San Remo dragged endlessly on: 'Here it seems to me more dull and depressing each day, nothing to do or see! Every morning I wake up and wonder and I am persuaded it will be like yesterday. I want, I need a change. I am getting too self-centred. I give way to a nasty temper, to depression and hate to speak of it.'

In January 1923 there was a wedding in Grasse. Olga's parents, still in mourning, declined to attend but Olga and Elizabeth went.

The best of Paris society was there and Olga and her sister were notable successes. They were shown off and included in every gathering over the long weekend: 'Not knowing anyone, it was of course very confusing at first.' By the sounds of things she enjoyed herself. On 20 February, Elizabeth and Marina left for the Tyrol and Olga stayed on alone at San Remo. March was a sad month for Olga; she was lonely without her sisters and to make things worse her terrier had to be put down. Life in San Remo was drab, though occasionally Olga managed to get away in the company of others.

One occasion was the funeral of Queen Milena of Montenegro where she met some of her more exotic Russian and Balkan relatives. Another was a trip to Monte Carlo for lunch with an uncle and aunt. Old Uncle Arthur, Duke of Connaught, was also present and he was immediately struck by the extraordinary looks of the young Greek princess. Olga was not to know it but it was thanks to the twinkle in his eye that her reputation as a beauty would precede her to London. And it was thanks to Aunt Toria (Princess Victoria, a sister of King George V of the United Kingdom) who had taken a great interest in her gorgeous young guest, that a visit to London was first proposed. Prince Nicholas and Princess Elena understood this was an opportunity to present Olga and, with any luck, secure her a future.

The long-promised trip to Florence at last materialized. The family stayed a wonderful three weeks in the Hotel Minerva and filled their days with visits to galleries, museums and palaces with Prince Nicholas, the erudite artist, as a guide. Financial consid-erations permitting, and with a fixed goal in sight, the family was heading to London for the season. Marriage season. 11 June 1923 was Olga's twentieth birthday and soon after this the family moved to London for the summer of balls and garden parties, and hopefully matrimonial opportunities. On 27 June, Princess Elena took her two oldest daughters to lunch with the King and Queen at Buckingham palace: 'Today, Mummy, Woolly and I lunched with the King and Queen at Buckingham palace. They were alone, he very talkative and rather noisy, she silent and shy! *Enfin* [finally] lunch went off all right and just before leaving they asked if we cared to go to Wimbledon to see the tennis matches, so he sent word to the secretary there who, on our arrival, came to meet us most amiably and took us to the royal box.'

Olga preferred outings with close friends and family rather than grand and formal occasions. For example, when invited to a ball given by Lady Zia Wernher she noted in her diary: 'On Friday afternoon we managed to go to the horse show which was marvellous but had to come away early to dress for a big ball given at Zia's house. There were over 400 people and being the first one and not knowing a soul made the whole thing an intense bore! David (Prince of Wales) was also there but didn't approach any of us.'

Olga had not enjoyed the ball, possibly because the stress of what was expected of her sapped any potential fun to be had, and it was with relief when on Saturday evening, '[Greek friends] asked us and U. Christo to the theatre to see *Stop Flirting*, a musical comedy – killingly funny. Shrieked with laughter the whole time.' Olga had no idea, however, that at the ball at Zia's house a gentleman had been struck by the graceful eldest daughter of Prince Nicholas of Greece. Unnoticed by Olga the young man stared at her for most of the evening. No doubt it would have surprised her to know that when he returned to his flat in Mount Street he was so affected by the sight of her he was unable to sleep; all he could think about was how he could arrange to see her again. After the rejection from Rico, and given her family's state of affairs, Olga would have been comforted to know there was a ray of light shining on her. From the very beginning the gentleman had noted her striking looks and innocence and had conceived the wild notion that she might make a perfect wife. HRH Prince Paul of Serbia was already in love with her.

THE WHIRLWIND

Paul had been visiting England for over a decade. He was popular with the society types and easily secured an invitation to wherever his princess could next be expected to show up. For her part, as we see in the following diary excerpt, she mentions him, so we know she noticed him.

∾

Tuesday night was the big Red Cross Russian ball at the Hyde Park hotel to which we all went. That same afternoon we lunched at Claridge's with the Alis (Alfonso of Spain and his wife Beatrice – the daughter of the Duke of Edinburgh). After that we had arranged to go to [...] see the polo, such a lovely place... [Paul of Serbia] sat with us...

∾

Paul danced with Olga at the ball and from her diary entry we see in her gentle references to him that she, too, seems to have made up her mind. They immediately seemed a team. When, through an intermediary, Paul invited Olga to watch the Prince of Wales at polo the following day, she readily agreed.

∾

Last night was quite amusing, especially watching the people. The host met us on top of the stairs with his sister who acted as hostess for him. Hotel is lovely with lovely pictures and furniture in it. David [Prince of Wales] was already there when we arrived and danced explicitly the whole evening with his lady love Mrs Dudley Ward. She has rather a sweet little face, and it seems she is very tactful (so Paul told me) and he likes her very much too. The Duchess of Sutherland was introduced to Mummy and has asked us on Monday to a fancy dress ball she is giving. Seems that only married ladies will wear masques and the girls something on the head. Today we are supposed to lunch at Claridge's with [...] and Paul and then... on to the polo.

TUESDAY, 17 JULY

For the Duchess of Sutherland's ball Paul chose the same fancy dress as six others, including his hostess. The Duchess, Paul and five others wore Japanese trousers with short jackets and big things on their heads with long masks! The Prince of Wales, needless to say, looked original and dashing dressed as a highlander. All, however, persevered.

On the following Wednesday, in the afternoon Paul came to fetch us to go [to the polo] for the third time. We lunched there but Puppy and Mummy had to leave at four to go to Buckingham Palace to tea... In the evening we all decided to go to the theatre at the last minute, just Puppy, Mummy, Paul and myself. We saw Lilac Time *with Schubert's music which was charming though very sentimental.*

THURSDAY, 19 JULY

Last night we went [out]. We didn't stay late as it was such a bore and not a single known person. Paul never appeared as he promised he would with the Duchess from another dinner party. We were back around one. Today I must stay in bed to be all right for this evening as we are going to see Stop Flirting *for Puppy's benefit. Paul is asking us and I am delighted to see it again! After that we go to the Portland's ball.*

∼

Each day there were machinations carrying on behind the scenes so that Paul and Olga could see each other: at the polo, at lunches, at dinners and balls. Paul even had the opportunity to show off his skills at the piano one night after dinner. At a garden party at Buckingham Palace, Olga witnessed Paul's general popularity and especially his friendship with the British royals. That her father, Prince Nicholas, evidently had a strong liking for her escort was hugely significant for Olga. The match appears to have been a fait accompli.

∼

MONDAY, 23 JULY

[The ball was] a bore as we knew hardly anyone. Poor Mummy had nothing but old men to talk to! As for myself I only danced twice with Paul and sat out the whole of the evening with him and didn't feel a bit bored.

～

By the end of that week Paul phoned to ask Olga out the next day. He took her to the cinema but he seemed preoccupied. Olga, correctly reading the scene asked, in a whisper, 'Have you found what you want?'

Paul turned to her and, with a look of gratitude, said, 'Yes, at last!'

The engagement became official on the Thursday when King Alexander's consent was received. Alexander's wife, Queen Maria, was expecting a baby in September so the wedding was fixed for Monday 22 October, to coincide with the christening. Paul invited the Duke of York (Bertie) to be his best man and invitations were sent out.

Olga went to Paris to prepare her trousseau and Paul made all the necessary arrangements from Belgrade. On Saturday 20 October, Olga arrived in Belgrade for the first time, accompanied by her family. The royal railway carriage had been sent to the border for them and Paul travelled to the penultimate station before Belgrade, to join them and tell them of the plans for both the christening and the wedding.

～

We drove to the new palace in open carriages drawn by white horses and the coachmen in powdered wigs! Alexander drove first with Puppy and then Mummy and Hellen (Mignon [King Alexander's wife Maria] being ill) then Paul and I, and lastly Arsen with Woolly and Marina. The others came by motor. On the steps Elisabeta [Princess of Romania] was waiting with Ileana [also Princess of Romania]. I was delighted to see the former again. When we had all assembled, we came upstairs to see Mignon who was in bed and looking much thinner in the face. Mana-Bell brought the baby who I found very sweet and not in the least ugly! We all had tea in the room next door and talked and neither of us knew from where to begin and what to say! In the evening there was a family dinner and just before, Bertie and Elizabeth arrived. After dinner they all went to the station to meet Aunt Sophie [Princess of Prussia married to Constantine, King of Greece]. After she came we all retired early to bed and poor Paul was simply dead with fatigue and emotion! We were living in the old palace in very nice rooms. Next morning at 11 was the christening. The baby was brought in a shut carriage drawn by six white horses in the arms of an old general and an old admiral. During the ceremony, which took place in the chapel of the old palace, Bertie and afterwards Aunt Missy [Princess of Edinburgh married to the King of Romania and mother of Maria and Elizabeth and Ileana above] held the baby. The ceremony over, Alexander took Peter with him to the window and showed him to the people. At 1 o'clock there was a tremendous lunch for 400 people to which the whole of Belgrade was invited, together with the foreigners present. In the evening there was again a family dinner and a gala concert afterwards. That night we none of us slept very much! In the morning Hellen came to tell us a few details about the service, then Sophica and her mother came in while I was dressing. Mummy came in to help me put on my veil. Just before starting to church she and Puppy blessed me with a holy picture which they gave me! At 12 the Minister of the Court came to say it was time to go so I took Puppy's arm and we walked along followed by the others. They were all wait-ing in the chapel when we came in and Paul was already standing in his place on the right in front of the altar. When the moment of the crowns came they were placed on our heads and left there and happily they didn't fall off! Bertie exchanged the rings. After the ceremony we went and kissed Puppy and Mummy then the rest of the family. There was a big lunch afterwards but less big than that of the christening. Then we sat and talked a little and I went to change for a short drive around the town, to show ourselves!!!! Then we came back and went to see Mignon and Paul took Mummy, A. Sophia, and me to see his rooms in which A. Missy was living those days! At six I came home with Puppy and Mummy to change as we were leaving at nine. I drove to the station with Alexander and Paul, the others following; they all came to the station except A. Missy and Elisabeta. After tender goodbyes to the family (I kissed Puppy and Mummy and sisters in the train) we slowly moved off… On our own life à deux! We had the same train as we came in. We got to Venice the next day at 11 at night feeling tired. We spent three days at the Danieli and on Friday morning we went to the station to see Puppy and Mummy who were passing through on their way back to Paris. We left that afternoon at 3 for Florence which we reached late at night. Princess Abamelek had taken rooms for us at the H. de la Ville. The next day Saturday we lunched with her at Pratolino and Paul took me all over the house and grounds which are enormous!

∼

After Florence they continued by train to Rome where for nearly five weeks they luxuriated in the vast Villa Abamelek. They saw the King and Queen of Italy and Philip of Hesse, whom they both liked. After three weeks Olga was able to write, 'our happiness, mine at least, increases daily and time seems to fly.'

This Italian sojourn could scarcely have been a greater change for Olga; particularly San Remo where, exactly a year before, she had idled as a frightened and lonely exile. Paul was at last not alone. They both must have felt saved from the yawning fangs of fate.

3

HRH Prince Paul of Yugoslavia: Part II

In 1921 the much-loved leader King Peter was ailing and at this point his title was, by necessity, perfunctory at most and his second son Alexander was already the Prince Regent of the Serbs, Croats and Slovenes. Alexander had grown up ready for this handover, had honed his every move in that direction, expecting to take over when the time was right. He was eager and he was groomed for the part, and had benefitted from an open dialogue with his father. From what I have read, however, neither of them ever included my grandfather Paul in their diplomacies or public affairs. They barely made a space for him in a civilian capacity.

Alexander fought fiercely in both Balkan wars and in World War I, and one of his first decisions as ruling prince was to commission a monument in memory of his fallen comrades. War was a splendid thing to him, a showcase of power and a time to feel pride. This monument would take more than a decade to complete. Prince Alexander's intentions for the monument incrementally expanded in size and magnificence, perfectly in step with his own expanding power grab from prince to absolute leader.

While my grandfather believed unreservedly in duty and honour, he had no personal fondness of violence. If anything he might have agreed it was a means to an end, but nothing more than that. His father, the famous warrior Prince Arsen, decorated for valour and devoted to swordplay from battlefields to private duels, was quite a different beast. He was more overtly Serbian one could argue; or just another type of Serb. There was always a coexistence of poets and artists in among the fearless Chetniks and *hajduks*. All of them were equally Serbian in personality.

That Alexander kept Paul at arm's length, politically speaking, was mitigated by his own lack of desire for power of any sort. He did not want to fight or rule. He was a private person and wanted nothing more than to have a family and live in safety. For his country he wanted to bring the refinements of culture; such were his simple goals. He did, in the end, achieve these goals: the museum exists to this day, although it is shuttered. He had the knowledge and the coin to gather the best. I look forward to throwing open those locked front doors and inviting one and all to admire his contribution. It will be a great day.

In the early 1920s Paul directed his energy to the world of fine art; learning and studying and gradually collecting. With no official job in Serbia, other than to show up sword in hand should war break out again, he was free to do as he pleased, and he made up his own rules as he went along. I wonder why he did not throw in the towel, move to Beverly Hills and date the prettiest actresses of the day because he could have. He could have been a playboy, he could have been a Howard Hughes, and yet, quite simply, it would never have occurred to him. He was trained in discipline and duty, he was trained to see Serbia as his responsibility and he never faltered from this, whether it appealed to him or not.

Despite his apparent footloose life, his objective was to settle in Serbia and do something beneficial for this country to which he was uniquely connected. It was not in his make-up to abandon ship. I almost wish he had, for his sake. But that was not who he was. And the more I learn about Serbs the better I understand him. He was Serbian, and that meant he was loyal to the end.

Paul's grand plan was to create a world-class art museum for Belgrade. All he needed from his cousin Alexander was the bequeathment of an appropriate setting, yet even this small detail became a source of contentiousness and irritation as Alexander said yes and then dragged his feet. In the late 1920s and early 1930s, Paul travelled around Europe almost continually on his own coin, burdening no one; he could play as he chose with his own immense fortune. He stayed in the villas of relatives in Rome and near Florence, or the south of France or Paris, and attended the endless parties of the English aristocracy. If there is one thing the British really love it is dressing up. They are all about 'proper' riding habits, and ball gowns and white tie, and garden party dresses and cricket whites and boater hats and Ascot horse-racing headgear of near comical indulgence. They are an eccentric people, but they would be the first to acknowledge this, no doubt with pride! An outsider, say a Wallis Simpson, would have been first and foremost judged on her wardrobe. Such are the Brits, God love them.

It cannot be overlooked, however, that Paul had no officially assigned residence of his own back in Belgrade, a point which was humiliating. Why was he not treated better and included? It was beyond insulting and unfair. His cousin Alexander frequently mentioned the possibility of this or that structure being made available for Paul and Olga, now a married couple with small children, though nothing ever came of these tantalizing discussions. But Alexander was not an easy personality to analyse. For one thing his relationship with his eldest son Peter was evidently and demonstrably cold and dismissive. The little boy – thin and cowed, with sloped shoulders and bowed head – was visibly affected by this harsh treatment. His father's critical eye seemed to weigh on the already jumpy child. The dynamic between Alexander and Maria and Paul and Olga was also a seesaw of mixed messages and paranoias fuelled by perceived jealousies and slights. A low-grade toxicity, real or not, it would one day corrode their fragile relationship with disastrous consequences. Olga notes in her diary her embarrassment at King Alexander's obvious preference for her first son Alexander (known by the pet name Schultz) over his own son Peter, which helped to encourage Maria to despise Olga and her children. Rumours spread of the fight for power between the couples; that Paul and Olga hoped to dislodge their cousins and grab the starring roles for themselves. Nothing could have been further from the truth. But rumours, spread by ill-intentioned enemies and saboteurs, are hard to dispel.

Despite Paul's constant travels and his lengthy stays at his Aunt Moina's delightful Villa Demidoff, he never considered putting down roots anywhere but Serbia. This country he was tied to was always foremost in his mind. The museum he tirelessly worked toward was for Serbia and, with the support of his beautiful young bride, he repeatedly hinted to his cousin Alexander of the need for a residence of their own. Paul and Olga had a suite of rooms at Dedinje, the massive marble royal palace complex, and they were welcome to stay for short periods, but their status as guests was wearing thin. They named their first son Alexander and his namesake uncle adored him. After many false starts a lakeside house in Slovenia was made available for them. Indescribably joyous and relieved at this turn of events, they immediately loved this place and made plans to fix it up. At last they could call somewhere home. Finally!

The house was indeed beautiful and they were enormously grateful. But consider, if you will, this was a thinly constructed house, only fit for summertime habitation. Furthermore, it was in Slovenia, a nation only loosely part of the Yugoslav experiment, and known to have more than a strong ambition for independence. In other words, one might easily – and quite suddenly – awaken in a foreign country. That sounds like the most passive-aggressive gift of all time; here's a home you can only live in half the year and at any moment it might ripcord free and you'll be abroad.

As King Alexander grew evermore autocratic on every front, Paul could only graciously muddle along with his peculiar life in the shadows and on the sidelines. To his credit, regardless of this ongoing disrespect at home, Paul's international reputation as an art connoisseur had reached the ears of the legendary art world superstar of the day Bernard Berenson, an American Jew with a global reputation for the finest eye in the business. Both these aesthetes – Berenson, with his own very magnificent Villa I Tatti, and Paul, with his relative's Villa Demidoff and the expectation of inheriting the Villa Abamelek, a mini-Vatican in its excess of splendour – instantly became friends. It was a friendship that would last all their lives.

King Alexander was making plans for the destruction of an ancient historical archaeological site at Avala which included the bombing of the mountaintop where there lay the unexcavated ruins of a Roman city. Meanwhile, Paul was constructively gathering up history in the form of Old Masters, mostly paintings. King Alexander and Queen Maria, and Prince Paul and Princess Olga had their respective broods of children, and in a way they coalesced as an extended family. Olga, who knew intimately how a close family acted, was not remotely fooled.

King Alexander was motivated by action and inspired to repeat the triumphs of his forebears with their legacies of military conquests, of commissioning impressive public monuments such as statues on mountaintops; grand gestures were his birthright. Paul, however, was a pacifist; an aesthete hunting for a good Tintoretto or Canaletto and collecting fascinating friends from among the top-tier intellectuals of the day. The cousins seemed so different: one a warrior and one a peace-lover, yet they were different sides of the same florin. They were both committed to their country and laboured on its behalf from differing angles, from a sense of predestined duty, in spite of their diverse approaches.

By early 1934 it was, at last, time to begin Alexander's masterpiece at Avala – the Tomb of the Unknown Soldier – and an explosives expert named Schultz was hired. Alexander was by now Supreme Leader and King of Yugoslavia. Instead of inviting his eldest son Peter to do the honours, he nominated his favourite nephew young Prince Alexander – son of Paul and Olga – to set off the dynamite and blow off the mountaintop of Avala.

1934–41

On 9 October 1934, King Alexander I was assassinated in Marseille. Prince Paul, who had never been given any official responsibilities, was only ever told one thing and that was, if anything untoward should happen to his cousin King Alexander, he was to immediately search the royal desk drawer and there he would find an envelope sealed with wax; therein he would discover heavily guarded secret instructions.

In his will – the fabled sealed letter hidden in his desk drawer – King Alexander stipulated that if he died by natural causes or any other manner before his eldest son Peter was officially of age, a council of three regents was to govern until Peter turned eighteen. The regents were to be one Serb: Radenko Stanković; and one Croat: Ivo Perović; and chaired by his cousin Prince Paul, my grandfather. Prince Paul, aged forty-one, accepted the regency.

In 1934, Alexander's son Peter was only eleven years old. Paul understood his duty and it would never have crossed his mind to do anything other than follow his cousin's orders. Overlooking the glaring fact that he was, for many reasons, wholly unsuited and unprepared for the post, it was his now, and he would see it through. I like to imagine my grandfather Paul checking his watch, and calculating it all out – Peter would turn eighteen in September 1941, and he must have reasoned it was not so very far off. I like to think he might have cajoled and consoled himself with the simple notion that seven years was not forever. He could do it. And furthermore, there was no question that he would fulfil this duty and then return to his life as a semi-civilian cadet of the realm.

In photographs of my grandfather during these years he is rigidly serious, wearing a white and gold brocade military uniform with sashes and ornate sabre and a cap. His back is as straight as a wall, his face impassive, inscrutable. In those photographs I think I see in his eyes a sense of consternation as if he knew he had somehow walked through the looking glass. Possibly he was counting the hours until this accidental freak show of 'running a country' would naturally come to an end. Perhaps it felt like falling into a Kafkaesque maze, but on the world stage; an Orthodox Christian accidentally scuttled into the Colosseum, surrounded by the hungry lions of the politics of Europe in the 1930s. Smart Jews were already emigrating to the United States. This was the time of Adolf Hitler's meteoric rise, and while admired by some prominent Brits and many smart types, he did not fool all of them; the prescient packed their bags and left. My grandfather, on the other hand, did not have this option available to him. And if he thought about it at all, he could go nowhere until September 1941; a date, I am quite sure, he looked forward to.

In 1936 Paul and Olga had a little girl who they named Elizabeth. After two boys, my grandmother was elated to have a daughter. This daughter is of course my mother Elizabeth – 'Pixie' as they nicknamed her – and she was a joy for her parents. She was a delightful and precocious brunette with enormous, soulful, dark eyes and a spirited personality. She was assigned a personal bodyguard, a soldier in the King's Guard named Mato Puketa, who was staunchly devoted to her. During World War II he stayed on and fought with the King's Army. He was shot at and one bullet hit its mark, so he was taken to hospital where the nurses fixed him up, and as soon as he could he escaped to fight with the Chetniks.

I have since had the good fortune to meet Mr Puketa's grandsons – Igor and Ivan Stojanović – and they tell me they remember seeing a photograph of their grandfather with my mother. Unfortunately the photograph is lost, but their memory of it is clear. For Mr Puketa's loyalist sentiments he was imprisoned for two years after the end of the war. I salute him and offer him my gratitude and my apologies for his mistreatment. Everyone suffered, and now, years later, the descendants can gather safely at the kafanas and toast our ancestors. It is small recompense for what our ancestors endured, and yet that we should now be acquaintances and friends, to me, is monumental.

Attempting to keep his attention on normal things, Paul pursued his plans for his museum, which he opened in the mid 1930s and this may have been the happiest time of his rule. Europe of the 1930s was many things to many people. The world was an interesting, fast-changing place. By 1938, as Paul's British acquaintances fussed over invitations to parties, my grandfather was presiding over the opening of the Tomb of the Unknown Soldier, his dead cousin's ambitious project. It was a forbidding omen at the best of times, and these were hardly the best of times.

That year my grandfather was on the cover of *Time* magazine, and the quote beneath his photograph, in which he looks deadly pensive and uptight in his military outfit, is: 'If only I had more time.' I can interpret this so many ways; none of them shine well on his 'allies', whom he was fast learning were not friends at all. He was, in their eyes, a pawn to be used, to be thrown to the wolves of the day. He could see the future and it was not bright. Still, he had no idea just how bad things were going to get.

In 1936 there was an assassination attempt on my grandfather – probably not the only one, but one I have documented proof of. It is typed up and stamped by a British government official proclaiming how they thwarted this attempt on Prince Paul's life. Why do the Brits have their fingerprints on everything?

I continue to hear that Prince Paul had political ambitions of his own, that he wanted to grab power from his cousin, the child Crown Prince Peter. I find this laughable. My grandfather wanted nothing to do with running a country. I have heard it said that when the time came for him to have to negotiate with Adolf Hitler, he had a 'vision' for his foreign policy. I say what tosh!

I do know my grandfather Prince Paul had no desire to be regent. He distrusted politicians and he disliked politics, but he was brought up with a strict code of conduct which included following orders. He had been ordered to fill the role of regent until young Peter was of age. I believe my grandfather accepted this obligation as a duty and while he surely regretted his bad luck, he never for a second thought of shirking the responsibility. After all, he must have consoled himself, it was only seven years and Peter would turn eighteen in September 1941. How bad could it be?

For my grandfather, to find out that he was supposed to manage Yugoslavia was a nightmare of an obligation. He wanted nothing more than to complete his duty and return to civilian life. Anyone who thinks Prince Paul was excited to be at the helm of this fractious country on the cusp of World War II is out of their mind! I find the timing suspicious that in 1939 Paul was installed as a Knight of the Garter, the highest British honour he could receive. Did these Brits hope to pull the wool over his eyes so as to deceive him into believing they were chums, great friends, allies; we won't let you down; just do as we say, keep a stiff upper lip and Hitler, oh, him, just play along.

My cynical eye reads this as a chit to remind the suddenly strategically prominent Paul of his anticipated subservience to mighty Britannia; Churchill and Eden specifically. With wealthier and far better militarily equipped countries worrying over Germany's flexing muscles, how could Paul, art lover and piano player, be expected to devise a foolproof plan to thwart evil Adolf?

Paul never wanted to attend a military school, and he never did. Nor did he wish to participate as a soldier in any war, and he never did. He showed up, as duty called; he wore his uniform but he did not engage in battle. He instead elected to be an emissary and take messages out of the country and off he went to Rome to stay at his cousin's villa, the Abamelek palazzo. Hardly the behaviour of someone looking to show off military skill and take control of anything beyond his own existence. He did not return to Serbia but instead stayed in England – in Scotland, in fact – hardly the front lines of war. And only because duty dictated as much, he joined his uncle King Peter in Corfu, where little Serbia was put to wait out the war. He did not wield a sword, but rather worked with the Red Cross. I ask you, are these the movements of someone salivating for power? Obviously not.

As Slav politicians debated personal nationalist interests, no doubt my grandfather had his eye on the clock, particularly September 1941 when young Peter would turn eighteen and take his rightful position as king. At that point Paul could resume his life as a civilian royal; he was eager to return his attention to his museum for Belgrade. How could he know it would all be snatched away forever? Hitler made his move on Poland and soon Germany was making demands directly of Yugoslavia. In response Yugoslavia declared its neutrality.

In 1939 Prince Paul, as acting head of state, reluctantly accepted a state invitation from Adolf Hitler and spent nine days in Berlin. My grandmother often spoke to me about this trip, and how Paul did not want to go. She showed me the photographs of him sitting in an open carriage with Hitler, and he is staring down at his hands, clearly deeply mortified and uncomfortable. She told me about the military parade put on to impress them, and how they noticed the same tanks and troops paraded past them three times – at least – to give the impression of greater firepower! They never let on that they noticed. There was an evening with Hermann Göring who was dressed up in a strange costume and made a point of telling her of his love for dressing up. My grandmother told me that one evening, after dinner, she cornered the Führer and asked him directly why he was not married. He replied, 'I am too busy for that. I am on a mission from God.'

After three years of delaying the inevitable, on 25 March 1941 Prince Paul allowed the Yugoslav prime minister to sign the Tripartite Pact. Two days later, with British backing, the Yugoslav army overthrew the government. It is family lore that my grandfather Paul was told he no longer owned anything and had twenty-four hours to leave the country or face a firing squad. Paul and Olga packed a few things, and with their daughter they left immediately for Greece. Their sons Alexander and Nicholas were already abroad. They made their way first to Olga's family home of Tatoi in Athens. But the Brits – Churchill and Eden specifically – deemed this far too cushy for them and so they could not rest for long. After making a phone call to seventeen-year-old Peter, who was now abandoned and terrified and in the hands of the 'powers', my grandparents were further condemned as 'saboteurs' and the British forced them on.

Quite astonishingly – and I have seen the internal memos that clearly outline these decisions – Anthony Eden and Churchill personally wanted Paul exiled to a remote island; like Napoleon was to Elba. No European country was permitted to grant them asylum. They could not go and live with their own family members scattered across Europe.

The Special Operations Executive files in the Foreign Office in London show the post-war communist authorities had 'Prince Paul proclaimed an enemy of the state'; he was 'disallowed from returning' to Yugoslavia and 'all his property was confiscated.'

The refugees first stopped in Cairo, after which they were soon forced to move to Kenya where they were held under house arrest by the British government in an unused lodge on the outskirts of Mombasa. The British, his friends! They were setting the rules and it was a horrifying time for Paul. He had lost everything on such a stunning level that it emotionally devastated him.

My grandmother often talked to me about their days in Kenya. We spent long, contented hours together in her townhouse on the rue Scheffer in Paris, and she told me about those extraordinary years, though not until putting together this compilation of research have I discovered how much she left out. She told me they were given a farmhouse in Mombasa. She said it was dirty and had not been lived in for a long time. She said they managed with the assistance of a few workers who spoke only Swahili. She told me that my grandfather slipped fast and frighteningly into a full-scale depression. He stopped eating, he stopped talking, he would only sit in a chair and stare into space, he closed himself off. My grandmother, the princess who was born in a palace, rolled up her sleeves and set about cleaning the filthy dwelling. She led the way with her retinue of local helpers and she showed them how she liked things. She went into the kitchen with them and together they all learned how to make dishes palatable to their European tastes. She also swiftly picked up Swahili so she could communicate with her team. '*Mass mali*,' she taught me to say, with a wave of the hand as if you're clearing smoke from of your face. '*Mass mali*'; it means, 'Take it away'!

My grandmother told me how she cared for my grandfather. I can never forget this image of her, sitting daily beside her morbidly depressed husband whose life had been shredded and his heart stomped on. In her gentle voice she would read stories to him and he would say nothing at all, but she knew he could hear her and she was his lifeline. She said this went on for years before he slowly began to emerge from this hardened shell, and gradually, ever so slightly, started to return from the shocking brink, slowly coming back to life – to love. My grandmother helped him over that chasm but she never told it to me that way. She told me the stories but she never made a martyr of herself. She talked about it as if it had been an unusual adventure, taking it all in stride, as if she was performing in a play. I would give her a standing ovation.

My grandmother also told me of an incredible journey, in the winter of 1942, to visit and comfort her recently widowed sister Marina whose husband, the Duke of Kent, had died in a plane crash. Overruling political obstacles, the British royal family appears to have played a role in making sure this could happen as Olga was the only close relative who could help the distraught Marina, her beloved little sister. This evident manipulation reveals, to my sceptical eye, the lengths and far reaches of political meddling.

Personally I rather wish my grandfather had flashed his middle finger to Churchill and Eden and moved to America, or the south of France, and relaxed into an appropriately comfortable carefree lifestyle.

Olga was allowed to make this visit because her other sister Elisabeth had married a German – not a popular nationality at the time – and their mother was in Greece. My grandmother frequently told me about this trip to see Marina, after years kept apart and unimaginable emotional hardship. The journey itself, during World War II, involved cold and uncomfortable military airplanes, and having to stop repeatedly as they refuelled across continents. The trip was arduous and it meant leaving her broken, frightened family in Kenya; yet she needed to be with her distressed sister whom she adored. My grandmother's choice was a double-edged sword of endless cuts of guilt.

Thanks to the intervention of Field Marshal Jan Smuts, the man at the helm in South Africa, in 1943 they were allowed to move there. I remember my grandmother mentioning this man Marshal Smuts and how grateful they were to him for his compassion and humanity. Here they stayed until 1948 when at last the restrictions on their personal movements were lifted. Paul first moved his family to Geneva. Then the French offered Prince Paul and his family a home when no other European country would grant them asylum; for this I am eternally grateful to the French.

It seems likely the ban was lifted at the request of the British royal family, because the change occurred after Paul and Olga met with King George VI and his wife Queen Elizabeth (once a potential spouse of Paul's) during their official visit to South Africa in 1947. I didn't know all of this when my grandfather was alive. While my simple childhood memories of him are clear and distinct, learning of his life story has been heartbreaking and I have cried and felt outraged frequently as I have typed this book. I only knew him as the formal gentleman with the steady, deep voice and the proclivity to laughter. I would never have guessed he had been through the jungle, emotionally.

After Geneva, Paul divided his time between Villa Demidoff and a townhouse in Paris. He never had any further desire to live in England, so to all those who call him an Anglophile I say look at the evidence. While he did admire them when he was an impressionable youth, later in life, after what he went through, his sentiments toward them never repaired. He was always loyal to his friends, and his family members, but the political team during the war years had personally attacked him and endangered the lives of his family, and he would never forget that. So no: he was no Anglophile.

The townhouse where they lived in the sixteenth arrondissement was pale grey stone, the colour of a dove. It was quiet and filled with a soft blue light that splashed from tall casement windows. My grandmother took her breakfast in bed while I ate mine in the dining room, served by Camille, the doddering, devoted butler. First, I would be awoken by gentle daylight after Marie, the maid of many years, pulled open the curtains. I would shuffle down to the dining room and Camille would serve me at a small table by the windows overlooking the street through gauze curtains, before leaving me alone with my toasted baguette and butter and jams. The room was subdued in greys and whites, with a large, round, highly polished table at the centre; the walls were hung with priceless works of art. I would sip my tea in a paper-thin china cup. By the time I returned upstairs to my room, the bed was made, my day-old clothes removed and a bath filled with warm water and ready for me to soak in.

I knew my grandmother far better than my grandfather because he died when I was a teenager. I had the good fortune to continue to see my grandmother throughout my twenties. After marrying my first husband, he and I lived in Paris for a stretch in a ratty studio in Montparnasse, and once a week I lunched with my grandmother at her house on rue Scheffer.

After many years the chef was ready to retire. My grandmother was apprised of this and was determined to go and say 'thank you' and 'goodbye' and asked me to accompany her. We walked slowly down the round stone staircase, through the dining room where the sound of crystal chandelier pieces tinkled and into the back passage where the light was harsh and the grimy recesses were centuries old. Here was another land altogether of darker grey stone passages and stairwells and we became lost. My grandmother had no idea where the kitchen was as she had never visited before. Her servants adored her, however. These servants were from a time when it was their honour, their privilege if you like, to look after the needs of the princess. Meanwhile they bowed and behaved obsequiously enough to make you believe in the fantasy too. Everyone played their role.

I remember a time we ventured into the attached garage where an old black car sat gathering dust, no longer used, the chauffeur long since let go, and my grandmother poked through boxes of ancient treasures. She gave me tiny books bound in soft leather with gold-edged pages, and from one a business card fell out. It was small and hard and it read very simply 'Prince Paul of Serbia'. We had a particularly close bond, my grandmother and I, and I am forever grateful for that. Olga was a huge influence on my heart and my health. We shared a passion for tiny things and we would play with her miniature bejewelled toys, some of which I still have as they somehow made it through endless upheavals. Long ago though, I stopped investing emotionally in objects, especially as they seemed too often to get lost in the chaos that was my own life.

In the front of the house, the only part I knew, glorious paintings hung on the stone walls, and the sitting room and dining room were full of Louis XIV knick-knacks and Napoleonic gold clocks and a special desk with inlayed leather and gold. On the table tops was the bric-a-brac of centuries of priceless gifts, the culture of a time long gone when any visiting relative exchanged delightful tiny treasures – enamel or golden boxes stuck with huge precious stones, little triptych panels of religious icons. There were also silver and gold and enamel photograph frames of black-and-white shots of another time, many taken by Cecil Beaton, and a large amount of Fabergé. What I saw was the tip of the iceberg, and I took it all for granted. In 1969 my grandfather sold Villa Demidoff, not only because the property had become too expensive to run properly, but with most of his resources repossessed by governments, the dream such as it was, had dissipated. The inexorable had long since begun.

My grandparents committed their last days to France, with frequent trips abroad. I picture them in the afternoon light, in their armchairs on the second floor, in the smaller, intimate sitting room, at the rue Scheffer in the sixteenth arrondissement. I miss them both and think of them with love in my heart and a gratitude for the time I had in their company.

Prince Paul died in Paris on 14 September 1976, aged eighty-three, and was buried in Switzerland. I was fourteen years old and in a boarding school on the south coast of England; a house mistress was given the duty of delivering the news. I remember the moment acutely. I remember the ugly sitting room with the worn sofa and this grave school employee. I loved my grandfather dearly, and was saddened and I remember I cried; a perfectly normal reaction. In retrospect, however, I realize I knew next to nothing about his life and after compiling this book my feelings for him have intensified with a deep respect and an equally deep regret for the treachery and indignity heaped upon his gentle soul, an experience of which he revealed not a trace. He never burdened any of his grandchildren with the sad details of his life; all he did was give us joy and love and I am so grateful for those memories.

On a personal note I feel compelled to add that I have heard Serbs call my grandfather an Anglophile, and it is clear they mean this derisively. Unquestionably, in his youth he did feel that way out of respect to a people who presented themselves as civilized to him in his chaotic younger years. But later, when Churchill and Eden personally turned on him, he never allowed them to poison his feelings for an entire nation. Nor did he lower himself to their shabby level. For example, he never spoke badly of these treacherous foes, neither publicly nor privately. Meanwhile both Churchill and Eden openly and intentionally dragged my grandfather's good name through the murk of propaganda and lies.

In 1939 the Brits presented my grandfather with a little shiny medal, the Order of the Garter. Did they hope to indenture him by impressing him with their domination? Why were they honouring him when their intentions were only to use him? Was it a passive reminder of who was the boss; a tacit reminder of what was expected of him: to toe the line, to do as they instructed?

Consider that in 1938 the Brits moved the widow Queen Maria and her two younger sons to England. Why? It surely was not her idea. Queen Maria was Romanian so why did she move to England? Was she co-opted? I believe so, and I also believe that too late she knew it. After all, what mother chooses two of her children and then abandons the eldest, leaving him behind in a country lost to civil war, unless perhaps she was directed to? Why would she choose to move to England when her native country was Romania and her adopted land Serbia? And how would she select a place to live out her years unless this place was made available to her? I have visited the archives at Columbia University in New York City where my grandfather's private papers are kept, meticulously organized and preserved in manila folders. How dare they play with the real lives of real people? 'Side-show' is the term Churchill used to describe Serbia in his memoirs of this sorry time in history.

From 1938 these corrupt politicians, Eden and Churchill, were already crafting their plan of action. Paul, their 'friend', was merely a tool in their eyes. I understand completely their constitutional requirements to put the needs of their own country first. But look how far ahead their plotting began and you see how deeply duplicitous and despicable their actions were. They tore apart a family, leaving little fifteen-year-old Peter in Serbia, setting my grandfather up for the fall of a lifetime. His loyalty and his self-disciplined sense of diplomacy and correctness had him silenced; he was strictly diplomatic, protecting the evil actions of his 'friends'.

Personally I have nothing against the Brits. I lived among them as a child, reared as I was in England, mostly London, and I made many decent friends there. My issue is not with them. I love their wit, their humour, their love of learning. I love their beautiful countryside and matchless stately homes. My issue is strictly with the politicians of the day, those who used my grandfather and who hurt him. It is them for whom I have no respect. One cannot blame the populace for the decisions of those in charge.

I suspect Winston Churchill and Anthony Eden were jealous of the handsome and exotic young Prince Paul from his early days at Oxford, with his immense personal fortune and his obvious search for a bride among one of their own. He courted the young Elizabeth Bowes-Lyon, the future Queen Mother. Later his wife's sister Marina would marry the Duke of Kent. Did they deem him and his ilk impetuous; foreigners come to steal from the finest in their own backyards? I can only hope they had more significant reasons for their behaviour toward my grandfather.

I am eternally grateful to the very shrewd Queen Mother who understood better than most in the British Establishment the difficulties my grandfather faced at this critical time. In April 1941 she wrote to former Foreign Secretary Viscount Halifax, 'I am sure you are sad, as I am, about Paul & Yugoslavia. I am sure he was afraid & perhaps weak, but with all his faults would trust him before any of these politicians.' These are sentiments she almost certainly conveyed to Churchill, who sadly did not listen. The Queen Mother remained a steadfast friend to Prince Paul and after the war they met numerous times. Until the end of Paul's life she treasured their time together.

It bothers me deeply that Churchill and Eden should so callously inflict their personal dislike on a person who intended them no harm and who stayed loyal to them despite their scheming ways. They forced him to accept an invitation to visit Hitler and you can see in the photographs of my grandfather in the open carriages seated beside Hitler that his eyes are downcast. I know, because my grandmother told me, that he was horrified by having to do this – he was very against it – but he went along with it. I wish he had not believed so deeply in duty. He had no desire for personal power; he had no desire to run a country. But he cared very deeply about the people of Serbia and he was intent on not being responsible for a bloodbath and the grotesque loss of lives. If visiting Hitler would win him time, he was willing to go along with it.

Consider how in his later years he never penned a memoir outing and maligning those who had almost destroyed him. He could have. Churchill never stopped writing memoirs, volumes of blather reinforcing his own belief in himself, perpetuating his personal myth. My grandfather was held back by his extremely good manners – I wish he hadn't been. I wish he had written it all and crucified them as they deserved. My grandfather was a gentleman to the end and Churchill and Eden used that against him. I wish he had broken from his own severe and strict upbringing and told them what he really thought, but that was never going to happen and they knew it; they took full advantage of it. And that is why, in 1938, a full year before World War II, all he said was, 'I wish I had more time.'

We all know it wasn't more time that he needed. And this quote demonstrates the depth of his sense of proper conduct, of diplomacy not propaganda. It was armaments, it was troops, it was military support that Serbia needed, not 'more time'. And without such help he could do nothing except unleash a bloodbath which he was not willing to do. He asked England and he asked America, and they said no, sorry, just hold Hitler off a while longer. Really? I ask you, what was the piano player supposed to do exactly?

But my grandfather, for all his genteel proclivities and love of art, was also deceptively resilient and patient and loyal and honourable, and I believe these traits are entirely Serbian. My grandfather's standing and good name were in tatters after Churchill's manoeuvrings; in Serbia as well as on the world stage. Today in the twenty-first century my mother, Princess Elizabeth of Yugoslavia, has worked tirelessly to restore his good name and I, too, with this modest book, hope to right some of the wrongs so unjustly inflicted on him.

After many years of dogged determination my mother achieved her life's greatest work which was to restore her father's good name; in 2011 HRH Prince Paul of Yugoslavia was reha-bilitated by the Serbian courts. On 6 October 2012 his body was flown from Switzerland and reburied at the family crypt at Oplenac, together with his wife Olga and son Nicholas. I kissed the cold white marble of their tombs, whispered prayers and could not stop the tears from flowing when I placed white roses over their gold carved Cyrillic names.

4

Karageorge

16 November 1762 – 26 July 1817

'Perhaps the liberty these men sought led them to cruelty in war and to lawlessness in peace, but this wild freedom was something for which all of them were ready to die. Among wild races a great man always has immeasurable influence, yet the true hero of the revolution is not Kara George, but the individual Serbian peasant. For Kara George is only the greatest, because the most typical, of these fierce sons of freedom.
[…]
The noblest aspect of the Serbian revolt is its universality. There was no recalcitrance and no treachery, yet there was no pay for those who fought, and every man who joined the ranks joined for love. Love of freedom.'

The History of Serbia
Harold W. V. Temperley

DELVING INTO THE HISTORY OF MY GREAT ANCESTOR HAS been a shocking adventure. As I look at him and explore the details of his life, I find myself becoming evermore curious. I hear myriad stories of how he was the 'cruellest of the cruel', and I hear tales of how he single-handedly slaughtered many hundreds of people. Was he a maniac? Was he the living embodiment of the myth of the noble savage? Or was this carnage in the name of freedom? Freedom from serfdom, freedom from oppression. At a time when Napoleon was earning glory for leading armies – and Europe was engaging in directly shifting the status quo – this ancestor of mine, Karageorge, walked off the fields he tended with his father and picked up a gun. He devoted his life to making a difference for himself and his fellow men.

I am told he was terrifying, ruthless, bad-tempered, quick to anger and just as quick to murder his foe. In modern parlance he might be considered a serial killer. Given the context of the time in which he lived he was a hero. Was he in fact a sadist, taking advantage of these circumstances? Or was he righteous and burning the devil with every shot he fired?

The more I learn, the more gripped I am as I try to answer these questions. I, however, as an American, grew up knowing next to nothing about him. It is the American way to look forward, and then suddenly I found it was time to look back, and look closely at this great man who launched a revolution, who overthrew the ruling authority of the Ottoman Empire and gained independence for his nation. For these extraordinary acts of courage Karageorge is known as the founder of modern Serbia and to this day, for his efforts, he is remembered with reverence. In Serbia everyone knows his name. That was never his goal, but that is part of his legacy.

If de Tocqueville and Rousseau and other great thinkers can agree on anything, it is that the ultimate job of the individual is to think beyond himself and the imposed strictures of conventional mores or laws and act accordingly for the greater good. Into this category, without question, Karageorge neatly fits and that is why his life and legend remain important. To scratch the surface of the tale of my great ancestor Karageorge is to enter a maze of confusion where even the spelling of his name or what exactly he looked like is up for debate. As for his heroism and the impact of his life's choices, these are indisputable. And for that I am not only grateful but extremely proud.

Regarding the details, however, no one, it seems, agrees on much, and this is because during his lifetime no one sketched him or painted him and by the time his likeness was composed for the mosaic at his tomb, he had been dead nearly a century. When I first visited the tomb, and for the first time examined his face, I decided I looked just like him, but of course this is sentimental tosh.

Everything I learn about him is almost immediately countered by a completely opposite suggestion and delivered to me with such a degree of intensity and certainty that I am left only with the clear impression that there is not one simple linear story to retell. I can only gather the threads of his legend and try my best to weave them into some sort of order. It will be impossible for any of us to ever know the exact truth, even about how tall he was; whom and how many he killed and why; what routes he travelled; and why he chose to return to Serbia, when he reached out for assurances of safety and was instead met with betrayal and death. There is no general consensus. The more people I ask the more variety I hear, except that these issues are in the background while his achievements stand strong. What I am discovering is pertinent, and that is why he is today the hero he was acknowledged to be during his own lifetime.

When I was a youngster I was aware of my Serbian connection but only in the abstract; for example, I never heard the language spoken and I was heartily discouraged from developing any desire to visit Serbia. My cousins and I were vividly warned we would be shot if we so much as set foot in the country. As for the founder of our dynasty, Karageorge, he was not much spoken of; and while of course I saw renditions of him and knew his name, I knew very few of the details of his life, including how he got that name, or even what it meant. Today I question why and I suppose it had to do with the cruel banishment of my family. My grandparents and their children were ignominiously chucked out and ripped away from all they had, including their young charge and cousin, Peter, only seventeen years old and more or less orphaned. When my family were commanded to leave their homeland within twenty-four hours or face a firing squad, they suffered enormous pain from which each in their own way never recovered. No small thing.

However, when I think about it, there was a great deal of merriment and mocking about a Serbian family called Obrenović. I never heard a first name mentioned, I never knew they were a 100-year dynasty that ended in a foam of bloodletting, but I knew the name Obrenović. I knew they were our sworn enemy, but that was all I knew. In other words, we grandchildren were 'radicalized' if you will! From a young age I knew that name, but I never heard my grandfather, Prince Paul, speak of it. Mostly these tales came from my mother and her older brother, my uncle Alexander, known in the family as Quiss. I clearly remember him talking about our Serbian family's enemy – the Obrenović family was spoken of derisively and laughed about. When we visited Uncle Quiss at his apartment in Paris, he often brought up stories about the enemy Obrenović. They were a known quantity within the family, while the feats of Karageorge were not, to the extent that should any of us ever encounter an Obrenović we should fight them to the death! This, in retrospect, is a strange dichotomy, but this is how it was. We were encouraged to have this opinion of a legendary enemy while at the same time there was no education about our great ancestor. I never questioned this when I was young. Now I do. And as much as I am interested in learning about Karageorge, equally I am convinced I do not wish to harbour ill will toward the Obrenović clan. These rivalries were relevant long ago, but they are not any more and I see no reason to perpetuate them. I only see meaning in bringing the entire story, sordid or not, into the light.

Equally, I remember my mother's frequent reminiscences of her early life at Beli Dvor, the beautiful palace in Belgrade, and her first years on Earth and it was always obvious she thought of that time as an enchanted era before everything got shot to hell. This is perhaps why the only words I ever knew in Serbian were Beli Dvor; I liked to joke that if I ever did visit Serbia that is what I would tell the taxi driver and it would be sufficient to take me home.

By contrast, I remember my grandfather's reticence to discuss anything Serbian; he never did. The history that we – meaning us grandchildren – heard was of our Russian lineage and our links to the royal families of Europe. My grandfather never displayed an ounce of temper, his mien entirely even, and, while loving and warm, he was also always reserved. The idea of questioning him about anything was entirely beyond imagining. If he talked about his past at all it was to do with his love of art and his beautiful Italian villa which he inherited through his Russian Demidoff side. He never once complained about his early life or even hinted at the troubles he had encountered, but what that also meant was he never explained himself. Conversely my uncle Alexander (aka Schultz) was quite different and the first to offer up jokes and tell funny stories; not about Serbia but rather about the Russian side – the Demidoffs – and he liked to make a pun of their name and laugh that it translated as 'half-tipping one's hat', but this was just to make us giggle. It was only much later on, researching this book, I discovered he had a very strong connection to Serbia. Raised there from infancy, he spoke the language like a native because he was in fact, quite unusually for a Karageorgević at this point, a native. He was even favoured by his uncle the reigning King Alexander.

It is entirely thanks to my grandmother HRH Princess Olga of Greece and Denmark, with her direct ties to long-established lines of royalty, that we were endearingly introduced to her Danish, Greek and Romanov heritage and to my grandfather's Finnish and Russian Demidoff ancestors and their exalted fortunes. My grandmother's side was filled with real fairy tales of palaces, shown to me in black-and-white photographs tidily compiled in albums. Less frequently, but also mentioned were the Grimm's fairy tale-like stories of assassinations and repeated exiles. Through marriage, we enjoyed intricate blood connections to all of the European royal families and everyone was referred to by nicknames and familiar truncations so that they seemed close and intimate even while they wore the crowns of Europe; for example, Queen Sophia of Spain, born a Greek Princess, was known affectionately as Sophie Spain. Our world was an insular, impenetrable cluster of codes and secrets. But I did not know anything else and it all seemed perfectly normal to me as I happily sat with my grandmother in her house on the rue Scheffer in Paris for endless cosy hours poring over her photo albums and absorbing all she cared to tell me. I loved her dearly and remember her with great tenderness.

In other words, there was inculcation in our past, our glorious heritage, but the emphasis was on everything other than the Serbian side. Wild Karageorge, or his descendants, I am sorry to say, were not spoken of much, if at all. His son and heir, Prince Alexander, was known to none of us. I never asked why at the time, but now I do. The simple answer is that Serbia represented a vast, unhealed wound in the lives and minds of my grandparents. It was a country to which my grandfather gave all of himself as best he could and was rewarded for this dutiful, unasked for position with his very life – and the lives of his immediate family – being threatened; the agony of national condemnation; the outright theft of most of his physical possessions and himself maligned on the world stage. Possibly, such tumult is more than any single human could bear, so he tucked it away and instead devoted his attention to that which gave him pleasure.

It is not until researching this book I noted that my grandfather Paul (Pavle) never once spoke to me of his own father, Prince Arsen. This Arsen, a man with an enormous and complex personality, was of increasing interest to me, and yet I don't think I even heard anything beyond his name ever uttered. His name was Arsen, but in the family he was always spoken of with the French pronunciation of 'Arsene'; again, no explanation was ever given. Swathes of information was kept entirely in the dark, redacted in a way so subtly and so profoundly I never even thought to ask.

The more I think about it, the more shocked I am that I had very little – to zero – curiosity. It was entirely by peculiar circumstances I visited Serbia in the summer of 2014, and on that first visit my concerns and my interests were centred on petty issues. So be it, they got me here – and for that I am grateful. Very quickly, almost immediately, and beyond my own sensation of a connection, I was witness to the reactions of the locals as they found out who I was. And who am I? That is a question that has dogged me persistently throughout my life. Yet in Serbia everyone seemed to know and more than that, they granted me a special dispensation. They accepted me as one of their own, which was a first for me. More importantly, everyone knew of my ancestor Karageorge Petrović.

Petrović? Even this I had never heard before. It was with delight I fell further down the rabbit hole into this rich other universe so full of stories and life and passion. I feel extremely lucky that, middle-aged as I am, I have the opportunity to have a second childhood where I meet an entirely new and very extended family. What a pleasure this is for me. Of my ancestors, Karageorge was previously a footnote to me. I see his forbidding intense mien frozen in portraits on walls in coffee shops, statues of him in parks, streets named after him, and on it goes. He is everywhere and I am encircled by his history and it pervades me. It has begun to influence me and affect my thoughts and feelings. My curiosity bloomed and instantly I wanted very much to know more, to know everything I could find out about him.

Best of all, every new detail I learned filled me with pride for this Serbian dynasty I had inadvertently neglected. The more I discovered the more joy I felt at the great honour it was to be related to such a fascinating family. People with principles, with innate morals and strong motivations and wild passions. People propelled by the desire to do good, to help their fellow man, to fight for what was right. It was a level of bravery and courage and discipline and altruism that startled me; so different was it from the soft excesses of the world I grew up in. I was deeply humbled by this and driven to learn. I stumble repeatedly in this investigation, but onward I go in search of more, no matter how contradictory.

For my purposes this story starts in 1804 – in the days of bloated, bursting empires – when this ancestor of mine George Petrović led a successful uprising against the Ottomans. Some say he was an illiterate peasant pig trader, others that he came from a noble family. Everyone agrees on some things and they are that he was uncompromising and ruthless, that his goals were just and pure. It has been pointed out to me that Karageorge, as the founder of my Serbian dynasty, was the 'cruellest of the cruel'. Not from my perspective; I see he fought for freedom and what greater cause can there be? The history of Karageorge would become legendary and grow after his death. His name and his exploits surfaced in the works of Pushkin and Hegel.

Darwin's theory of evolution is based on a principle of variations. The more I find out about Karageorge the more I see myself. I am quick-tempered, rash, violent, humorous, fair, thrifty, honourable and spartan. Yet he was a warrior and I am a writer, he was a giant and I am small, and on and on go the many other evolutionary adaptations. I look at the sword and I pick up the pen, and I do not know which is the mightier, or the more worthwhile. Perhaps it is not for me to judge.

Only vaguely through my early childhood was Karageorge referred to, and only in the scantest overarching way. That he existed at all was about as much as I knew. My lineage was so fractured that he seemed a very small part of things. On the Oxenberg side were American Jews from Russia and on my mother's side there was all of Europe with kings and queens and massive fortunes; I even knew of our direct links to Genghis Khan, all of which made us very proud. And then there was this detail of a wild and savage warrior, Karageorge, from a country where we were not welcome. I was told 'Kara' translated as 'black' but I did not know it was a Turkish nickname; I knew the man was revered, but I did not know exactly why. Besides, attention was elsewhere – on the Russian ancestry – and this is how he so easily became marginalized to us, his very own descendants. Therefore, I would have to say that while I knew we were somewhat Serbian I knew next to nothing about the founder of our dynasty.

I will add, however, that when I learned of his many murders, and specifically that he may have shot his own father to death with a bullet in the head, and had one of his brothers hanged, none of this shocked me nor offended me. It does not cloud my opinion of him. For one thing, royal families through the ages – from the Pharaohs to the Tudors – have locked each other up in towers, fatally poisoned one another, and gone so far as to order beheadings of rival siblings, cousins, fathers and sons with ambitious stepmothers looking to promote their own children. None of this is new. And in the histories I have read the reasons were for personal gain, for personal advancement; in other words, greed.

❧

'...the wild elemental natures, so often found among the savage peasants of the Balkans, cruel yet heroic, wild and yet generous!'

The History of Serbia
Harold W. V. Temperley

In the case of Karageorge his reasons were either to protect the lives of his family, sacrificing one for the good of his tribe, or because of a breakdown of decency. Karageorge acted harshly, but from a sense of justice and never simply for his own gain. Therefore, to me, his actions are not only explicable, but honourable. Some people might call his mass murdering barbaric, but I say closely examine his reasons and then ask just how barbaric is it to punish the bad and save the good?

My impressions of Karageorge were mostly misguided and incorrect and glossed over to such a degree I did not even have much curiosity about him. It was only after first visiting the country, and most specifically visiting Topola and the family crypt of Oplenac, that the significance seeped quickly into my imagination like liquid nitrogen and blew it open. I realized, once the information was presented to me, that I was fascinated with this individual – Kara George, Black George, Karageorge. Even his name was bewilderingly intriguing. I found him infinitely interesting and the more I learned the more proud I was of his actions and his legacy. I had not expected this.

In retrospect I realize I grew up feeling I was from everywhere and at the same time nowhere in particular. While I am American by birth I was raised in England and, with my closest cousins, who were half-Italian, I spoke French. Some of us were Orthodox Christian while others were Catholic. None of us had a single national identity that bound us, or that we might easily have cleaved to. However, it seems to be human nature to desire heroes to revere. I, too, wanted to believe in something and from a young age I discovered the stories of ancient Egypt and the Pharaohs and Isis and Osiris and they affected me, lit my imagination. I read all I could about this a long ago time, and I fervently wished there was a link to me. I was maybe ten years old at the time. Next, I pored over the works of Thomas Hardy and identified with the torrid sadness of the heroes of his stories, and onward I went to the explorers and the outcasts, such as maligned Heathcliff and on through the dramatic, impassioned, righteous Russians and then fell hungrily upon *Candide* and the rest of Voltaire's philosophies. It was in literature I found my heroes. When I look back I see it was crucial to me to believe in someone, if only through the words and thoughts of others, but I never noticed that any of them were real people from history. I was searching, but on another plane.

Next I came across a book about Abraham Lincoln and could not help admire him for the big gestures and grand strokes he was most famous for; but equally for his passion as a child, his dedication to an education of his own, despite his family barely having the wherewithal, and how at night he read by candlelight; such was his determination to clear the obstacles in his way. There was no trace of barbarism in it and today, as I attempt to compare Karageorge to the heroes of my youth, or even anyone I might still admire, I think he is closer to a superhero, an infinitely courageous rebel both dangerous and impossible to deter; yet always righteous and selfless – someone beyond the reach of negotiation, someone who has no price, who cannot be bought. All this makes him deeply interesting to me. He was not vain yet he had epic goals. I read somewhere he said he would rather die than live as a slave. His ambitions were never corrupted by personal greed.

I felt the need to write this book because I never heard anyone talk about Karageorge and I do not wish this darkness to perpetuate. I am appalled to admit no one I knew in America had heard of Karageorge. In fact, they mostly have no idea where Serbia is or that the country even exists. If I have ever tried to share my knowledge of this history, their eyes glaze over with lack of interest and boredom almost instantly.

When I first visited Serbia, I wondered if I carried any traces of my Serbian origin. I found out very quickly I had misidentified myself all these years. I had noticed I was loud, I was aggressive, I was obstinate and stubborn, I was easily enraged and yet equally passionate about that which moved me or anything I loved. I was physically strong and unafraid and the first to accept a challenge. I noticed these traits and I mistook them for my American side.

Up until my first visit to Serbia, I had considered Karageorge unimportant, but then I realized that everyone in Serbia knew who he was and what he stood for. When I first visited the country I was thinking not at all about Karageorge and barely about Serbia. Serbia was less a reality for me and more of an emotional hot button. It was a place I felt rejected by and confused by; a place I expected not to like because I felt a sense of connection only to the pain I knew my grandfather had experienced – the devastation he went through when he was thrown out of this country – so in all honesty if I had any emotion at all it was a certain sense of outrage. And it was not until I was physically there that these ideas not only melted away but were replaced by a sensation of relief and joy – a desire to belong and stay and learn – and perhaps I even felt a certain embarrassment at my misconceptions and prejudgments and wanted very much to correct them all.

Just like my great ancestor, I confess I have a horrible temper that flares easily and consumes me to the point where I cannot see straight and I am engulfed with rage and the need to set things right; 'right' being a vague idea and muddled with desires for retribution. Just as quickly my temper, once exploded, is gone like a tropical storm that flashes and is soon replaced by bright sunshine, the only traces being the teardrops winking from branches. My own mother, too, has this volatile temper and as a child I was never sure what would make her laugh and what would set her off. Naturally I always tried to make her laugh, but sometimes I missed the mark and she exacted her own style of retribution. Sometimes she broke hairbrushes on me, in a rage. Other times she clapped her hands and egged me on when, in the middle of her cocktail parties, I donned my flamenco dress (I had two), snapped my castanets and entertained her guests. Sometimes she encouraged me, other times I annoyed her; I just never knew which way things would go, but it was so much fun to see her laugh – it was always worth the gamble. More important than her temper, which may possibly be a Karageorgević trait, is her courage and fearlessness and for that I admire her reverentially. My mother, in the past fifteen years of residency in her homeland, has responded every time a national emergency presented itself, from floods to the needs of children. She has worked hard to rehabilitate the good name of her cruelly maligned father, Prince Paul. She has had streets renamed in his honour and she has promoted his work regarding his museums and tried to continue and fulfil his visions with regard to the arts. For all this I applaud her efforts and her achievements. My mother is an impressive and substantial Serbian and her contributions inspire me as I know they inspire others. She is respected and loved in Serbia, and she deserves this. *Chapeau Mama!*

In superficial ways my mother and I not only look very much alike, but our personalities are similar. Yes, she and I both have stormy, passionate tempers; and yet we are the first to laugh, the first to give, and I believe we share a sense of purpose and duty that is simply innate. I see her now, returned to live in Serbia, the country where she was born, and I see her great joy at coming home. I know she feels connected in a way she never has before. Christmas came late for her in life, but it is immensely gratifying to see her content and at peace at last. It is good to see her feeling at home after a lifetime of exile.

On the other hand, I never saw any display of temper in my grandfather. He would tell funny stories, but I never heard him raise his voice, or lose patience, or even show a hint of anger. That is not to say he did not feel very deeply, only that he had better self-control. I attribute this to his childhood and all of his teen years which were the antithesis of both my mother's and my own. My mother was feral in Africa, with a mongoose for a pet, and I was squirreling away in tiny spaces in my house and turning them into forts, just for me and my make-believe worlds. My grandfather, by contrast, experienced a massive dose of discipline in his childhood; first emotionally orphaned and physically abandoned and later, in the company of cousins, raised in a strict military court. He learned very young how to disguise and control his feelings – at least on the outside. For sure, his own father, Arsen, was rather out of control and only liked to spend his time signing up for wars, or gambling and drinking and womanizing, and was never remotely interested in bland domestic life. It is only after pursuing the research for this book that I see the issue of Karageorge's temper and its irrefutable genetic implications. I am not proud of my temper and I wish I could control it more than I can. I have often said that if I had been born a man I would be in jail long ago for manslaughter at the very least. Now I know where I get it from, I understand it better, even if I still cannot control it.

During my childhood and early youth, I attended fourteen schools – mostly in England, but also one in Spain and three in America – and Serbia wasn't mentioned in any of them, let alone Karageorge. His legend was never a part of any school curriculum that I was introduced to, and I attended a great many schools. It was non-existent, I am sorry to say; all the more reason for this book to be printed not only in Serbian but also in English. It will be my pleasure and my life's greatest purpose if I can breathe renewed life into this story and carry it abroad. After all, everyone is always in pursuit of truly inspiring heroes. Karageorge was the real thing!

When I saw all the monuments in honour of Karageorge, I was overwhelmed. I was stunned. I had no idea who he was, how important he was to Serbia; the breadth of his legacy. I was, in a word, shocked. But it only fired up my curiosity and made me determined to learn all that I could, and that is what set me on this current path which then led me down many more half-lit pathways into the confusion of his story and the variety of 'truths' about him. There does not even seem to be a consensus on how his name should be spelled. Again, this is trivia compared to why he is remembered in Serbia today. The actions of Karageorge and the legacy of those actions inspired a nation to shrug off the shackles of 500 years of Ottoman rule.

I knew none of this before visiting the country. I was somewhat stupefied by the 'cruelty' I repeatedly heard about, and yet at the same time I felt pride in him because in my understanding he was not needlessly cruel, but rather he was exacting in his version of justice. He was motivated by an attempt to correct what he saw as wrong. Instead of being mortified by this 'cruelty' I feel compassion for his need to do what he believed was right, regardless of the consequences. As to his heroism, I think it only proves that what was seen as cruel was instead necessary. Otherwise he would not be considered a hero; he would be considered a serial killer. But obviously, as is expressed by the people of Serbia and their attitude toward him, his 'cruelty' was a harshness appropriate to the time in which he lived and in response to the obstacles which surrounded him. His brutal end – a beheading – I only learned about due to researching this book. Initially I was horrified and saddened. I was affected on a primal and physical level. It made me wince and I thought it grossly unjust given his motivations. However, I suppose if I think of it calmly I see it might have been an inevitable end for a life lived quite so uncompromisingly. You live by the sword, you die by the sword.

I am told that the Serbian collective memory of Karageorge's murder was the source of internal division for the next two centuries, and that even today Serbs are virtually divided into supporters of the Karageorgević or the Obrenović dynasty. In response to this I can say that while my childhood was somewhat bereft of information regarding Karageorge, there was a certain amount of banter about the Obrenović family, at least from my mother and her older brother Alexander. That these Obrenovićs were our enemies and that we were encouraged to hate them and speak derisively of them, despite our scant knowledge, is of interest to me now. I knew the name and I knew they were the 'opposition', but when I examine the facts I see they were equally brave and equally motivated to see their country in better circumstances and I was obliged to open my mind and let go of my early muddled training in order to see them as real people with more to the picture than I was aware of. I refuse to hate them any more, and I think the only way forward is to embrace and put down these swords of misinformation. That the first Obrenović was responsible for Karageorge's murder is hard to negotiate with, but the descendants cannot be a target of hatred forever. That to me seems useless.

Perhaps in the history written in the nineteenth century or early twentieth century Karageorge was a recognizable, if remote, figure. Sadly, today, I do not hear him mentioned at all which is all the more reason to write his story and reintroduce him. He should not be forgotten. He is not forgotten in Serbia so now we just have to inspire the imagination of the rest of the world to take an interest in him. And if a Hollywood blockbuster was to be dedicated to his memory, who should play him? I really cannot say! More important to me is that they get the story right.

THE HISTORY OF KARAGEORGE

'The Serbian peasant was one of the hardiest of men, enduring, seasoned to all weathers, patient and fearless.'

The History of Serbia
Harold W. V. Temperley

Karageorge was born George Petrović on 16 November 1762 in the village of Viševac, Šumadija, south-central Serbia – an area of forests and mountains. Pig trading was the common industry of this region and the Petrović family, just like all of their neighbours, were ordinary swine herders.

Finding out that I come from the land of pig traders I cannot help but wonder if my own love of prosciutto might be hereditary. Learning this detail I laugh because for many years I have thought of prosciutto as the food of the gods. I have long wondered if cavemen ever dreamed of a future where meat sliced so thin you can see through it would one day exist, and become a staple of man's diet.

Two hundred or so years ago, this pig industry was a simple matter of allowing the animals to wander about, feasting on fallen acorns from the many trees of this forested area, thereby, with minimal outlay, making the business easily profitable. Sure enough, as is the way with farming of any kind, people began to clear the forest to make new space for more animals. As the forests were cleared, less natural food supply was available, thus the feeding of the animals became an expense where before there was only profit. The balance of favour gradually tipped against those doing the work. This hardship was just one of many issues that bred discontent. Thus the people were increasingly faced with the need for personal sacrifice and penury and this, added to the indignities of taxation from overlords, was one of the backbone issues of dissent.

Young George had four siblings: two brothers, Marko and Marinko; and two sisters, Marija and Milica. His father was Peter Jovanović and mother Marica (née Živković). George was no doubt inspired by the zeitgeist of crumbling empires. Despite coming from a family of farmers he was quite naturally a born warrior and his inclination for justice was innate. Apparently he could neither read nor write. He had no interest in the refined arts of civilized life, and yet it is possible he and his brethren caught news of Napoleon and his glorious pursuits, of the recently beheaded French ruling class. George's father was known to be a man of peace, some might consider him meek, yet George was by nature predisposed to question authority, he bucked obstreperously at the indignities he witnessed imposed on him and his people by the Ottomans and their vassals – the Janissaries. While his father tried to hold him back and teach him tolerance, George would have none of it and stood up to these Turks, repeatedly engaging in often lethal spats. Legend has it this is how he gained himself the nickname of Karageorge. Some say it was due to his swarthy countenance but just as likely, if not more likely, it was due to his unforgiving personality.

According to one professor the correct spelling is Karađorđe, but when I argue that this is not the Latin alphabet as agreed upon by the rest of the world, there are suggestions ranging from Kara George, Kara Đorđe, Karageorge and Karadjordje and that is just his name. The ending of all Serbian names is 'vić', meaning 'son of', like Johnson. Therefore for his descendants the name became Karageorgević (as my mother Princess Elizabeth of Yugoslavia spells it) and the spelling options of this go on almost indefinitely. Besides all that, there is Cyrillic.

The spelling of this name has morphed into today's pile-up of options and is a bedrock of incessant arguments. Almost all the members of my own family, whose name it is, spell it differently. To find out that the family name, if one is to be a purist, is Petrović, is quite a surprise. Certainly easier to spell and pronounce!

During his early life George worked alongside his father, the two of them available for hire as labourers. Petrović senior was a peaceable man and he noticed early on that his son was of quite a different temperament and tried to reign him in. This would prove futile, and eventually even deadly. George was frequently tangled up in disputes and these disputes inevitably involved interactions with the despised Turks or their representatives and the results ended either with a dead Turk or with George in mortal trouble, or both.

Where did this streak come from? Not his father, that much is clear. George was huge, he was fierce; he was easily enraged. People, both his enemies and his supporters, feared him. He loved to drink, he loved to fight, but there were also times he would sit alone, sometimes for hours on end, not speaking a word. Where did these traits come from? Was he a barbarian? If you listen to the stories you might think so. Or was he merely a product of his time, responding in a Darwinian manner to the needs of the day? Change occurs, stasis is never the status quo, not for long. And yet, there was little incentive to stand up to the ruling classes. Those who dared ended badly; some were impaled, others executed. Exhibitions were made of these upstarts' efforts. George, however, would not be deterred.

When he was twenty years old, George met his future wife, Jelena Jovanović, and I have heard it said he loved her as much as he feared her. Perhaps she was the only person in his life he ever felt this way about. Despite sometimes years of separation he was always true to her, as she was true to him. They settled in the village of Topola, equidistant from their home towns, in central Serbia. Karageorge and Jelena had four girls: Sava born in 1793, Sara born in 1795, Poleksija born in 1797 and Stamenka

Coronation of King Peter I,
St Michael's Cathedral, Belgrade,
21 September 1904

Prince Arsen, Prince Paul and
King Alexander, Belgrade, 1920s

King Alexander I with Princess
Olga and her sister Princess Marina
(future Duchess of Kent)

Young Princess Aurora Demidoff

PLOT AGAINST PRINCE PAUL.

" A plot to assassinate
PRINCE PAUL OF YUGO-SLAVIA,
head of the Yugoslav Regency Council,
and brother-in-law of the Duchess of
Kent, was foiled by the Belgrade police
according to reports from Belgrade, this
week.

A number of arrests were stated to
have been made in the capital".

Portrait of,
PRINCE PAUL OF YUGO-SLAVIA.

Portrait of Prince Paul accompanied by a report of a conspiracy
and failed assassination attempt from January 1936

Prince Regent Paul and his wife Olga and three children, c. 1939

Prince Paul next to Adolf Hitler on a visit to Germany, June 1939

Princess Olga wearing her tiara. Taken during Prince Paul
and Princess Olga's visit to Buckingham Palace, July 1939

Princess Olga, King Peter II, Prince Regent Paul,
Royal Palace, Belgrade, c. 1940

King Peter II

King Peter II, Queen Alexandra and
Crown Prince Alexander, c. 1948

Princess Elizabeth, Metropolitan
Museum, New York, 1959

Princess Elizabeth and daughter
Catherine, New York, 1962

Christina and her mother at a party for
Christina's book *Taxi*, New York, 1986

Christina in Paris

Crown Prince Alexander and
Crown Princess Katherine, Belgrade

Christina and her mother, Los Angeles, 1988

KARAGEORGEVIĆ FAMILY TREE

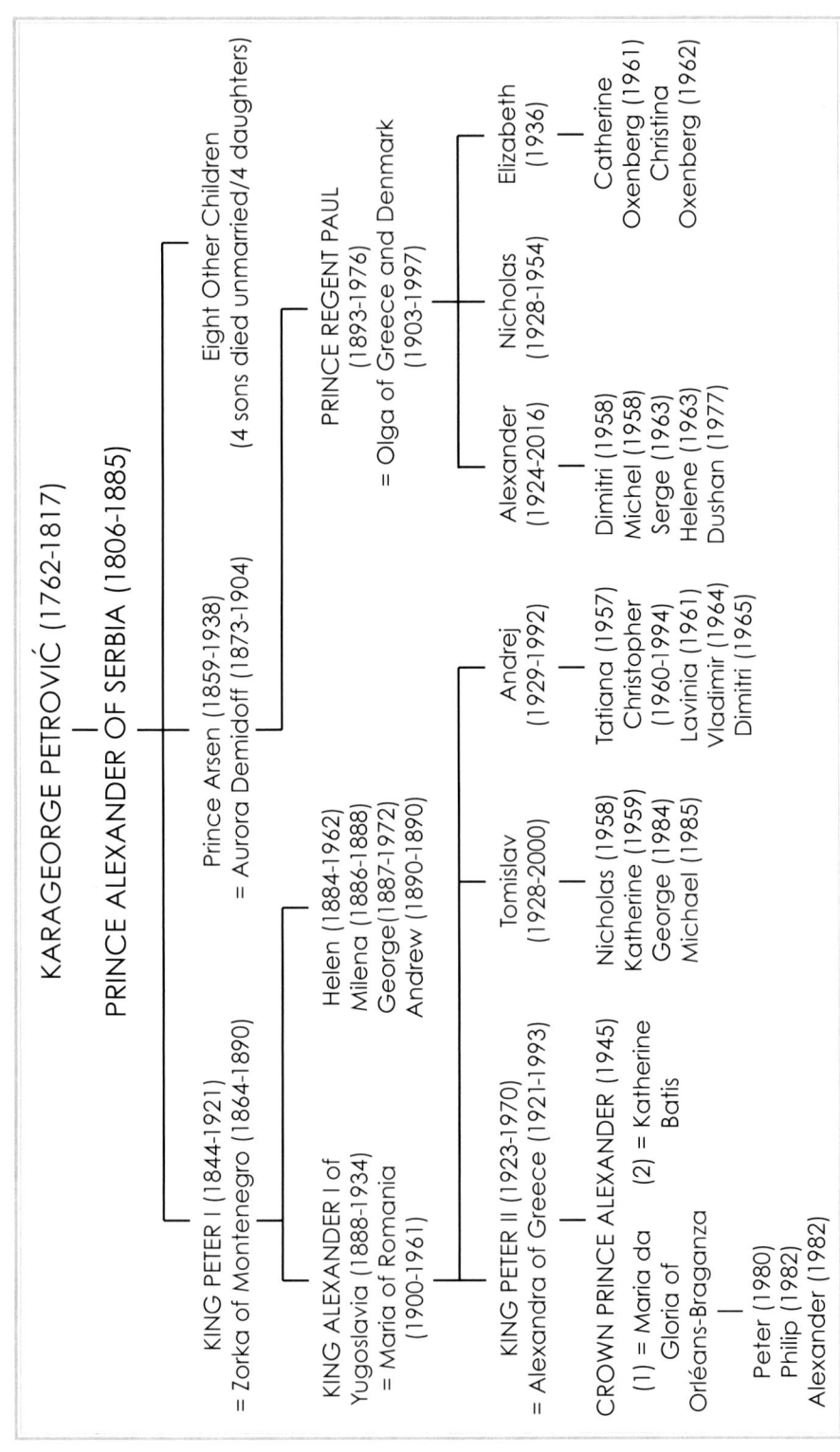

KARAGEORGE PETROVIĆ (1762-1817)

PRINCE ALEXANDER OF SERBIA (1806-1885)

Prince Arsen (1859-1938)
= Aurora Demidoff (1873-1904)

Eight Other Children
(4 sons died unmarried/4 daughters)

PRINCE REGENT PAUL
(1893-1976)
= Olga of Greece and Denmark
(1903-1997)

Alexander
(1924-2016)

Nicholas
(1928-1954)

Elizabeth
(1936)

Dimitri (1958)
Michel (1958)
Serge (1963)
Helene (1963)
Dushan (1977)

Catherine
Oxenberg (1961)
Christina
Oxenberg (1962)

KING PETER I (1844-1921)
= Zorka of Montenegro (1864-1890)

Helen (1884-1962)
Milena (1886-1888)
George(1887-1972)
Andrew (1890-1890)

KING ALEXANDER I of
Yugoslavia (1888-1934)
= Maria of Romania
(1900-1961)

Tomislav
(1928-2000)

Andrej
(1929-1992)

Nicholas (1958)
Katherine (1959)
George (1984)
Michael (1985)

Tatiana (1957)
Christopher
(1960-1994)
Lavinia (1961)
Vladimir (1964)
Dimitri (1965)

KING PETER II (1923-1970)
= Alexandra of Greece (1921-1993)

CROWN PRINCE ALEXANDER (1945)
(1) = Maria da   (2) = Katherine
Gloria of   Batis
Orléans-Braganza

Peter (1980)
Philip (1982)
Alexander (1982)

born in 1799. Karageorge and Jelena reportedly also had a son born in 1788 who died in early childhood. They continued until they produced two more boys: Aleksa, born in 1801, and finally Alexander, born in 1806 into a brand new Serbia, a liberated Serbia. It would be little Prince Alexander – despite being their youngest child – who would soon be singled out as the natural heir.

After one too many conflicts – specifically the killing of a Turk after Karageorge saw this man humiliating one of his own men – he became a hunted man. Karageorge knew for his own safety and the safety of his family that it was time to leave the country and get far out of the reach of his enemies.

Here the story confronts one of its many conflicting tributary options – the killing of his own father. One version goes that late one night Karageorge organized his parents, his wife and his children – laden with all they could carry – and began a trek, heading for the relative safety of the Austro-Hungarian controlled Military Frontier. To reach this swampy forest they would have to cross the Sava River from Serbia into Austro-Hungarian land. This area today is known as New Belgrade and built up with high-rises, wide boulevards and mega shopping complexes. But in those days it was a boggy, dangerous and wild land. Right there on the Serbian side of the river Karageorge's father attempted to deter his son's escape plan and in response Karageorge shot him in the head. Another version is that his father threatened to turn his son in to the authorities before the trip had even begun and Karageorge shot him right there and then. Another version has it that this was not his biological father, but rather his stepfather. What is agreed is that Karageorge murdered whomever it was who attempted to talk him out of his plans and block his path to safety. After the shooting, Karageorge went ahead and removed himself and his family northbound.

If you stand on the southern riverbank of the Sava River today and look northward to the other side, you will see the treacherous, ominous marsh has been tamed into a city. It is the playground of the young and the riverbanks are crowded with flat, wide boats, brightly lit like party lights and devoted to music and drinking and the careless concerns of frolicsome youth. Karageorge could never have guessed at the transformations ahead. All he knew at that time was he needed to secure the lives of his loved ones, and this is what he did. They crossed the river and next he settled his family somewhere and then he moved alone into Krušedol Monastery where he would stay for the next few years, waiting for the right time when it would be safe to go home. And so began the legacy of the exile of the Karageorgević clan. This was the first of what would turn out to be 200 years of moving back and forth, in and out of Serbia, into safety and away from mortal threats.

While Karageorge was illiterate and had no interest in the soft arts of reading or writing, the art of war fully fascinated him and he was intent on fighting. While he lived at the monastery he volunteered for the Austro-Hungarian forces, fighting in their legions made up of foreign fighters. He fought with them against the Turks and anywhere else they would have him and as he honed his skills in warfare, soon everyone who saw him agreed that he excelled. After several years of warring, and long after his wife and family had returned to Topola, he, too, eventually went back to his home and his domestic life of farming and pig trading.

When he was back in Topola he was soon known to all as the ruthless man everyone came to admire and fear. I can imagine that if he had no enemies to fight he would have waged war on all living forest creatures as viciously as any opposing army, thus he would likely earn a tidy living trading meat and skins to the insatiable and wealthy Austrians.

But there was always a fight to engage in. Serbia, after all, was not independent, and Karageorge adamantly believed it deserved to be. When he wasn't farming and marketing his livestock, he would join the brigands in the mountains and fight alongside as a guerrilla, a *hajduk*, with other intrepid rebels. One such was his Serb comrade Miloš Obrenović, a man with whom he would later share many years of misery. Karageorge was a natural fighter and leader and the people who fought with him respected him, but more than that they feared him and his legendary quick-hot temper. I am told he was massive in stature, wore his hair in a long untidy ponytail down his back, that his sword was always at the ready and he was not averse to strangling a person he deemed unworthy of life.

I have seen a grey stone statue of Karageorge in the park in Vračar, intended to commemorate the spot where one day he and his followers would set up an army camp from which to storm fortified Belgrade, and the statue has him carrying a sword with a curved blade which is half his height. Not a man to toy with, by any means. Most importantly he was motivated, rightly or wrongly, by his concept of justice. He was ruthless but he was also righteous. He did not kill for the fun of it and, in my opinion, he was not a psychopath. But he certainly was dangerous and this legend abounded during his own time and stands to this day. For example, when Karageorge heard the news that his younger brother Marinko had accosted a young girl – some versions of this episode say Marinko raped the girl – without hesitation

Karageorge had his brother hanged. What is not contested is the fact that Marinko lost his life at the insistence of his intractable brother Karageorge.

At the turn of the nineteenth century, after generations of toeing the line, the Janissaries – the Ottoman-created military class – had begun to splinter their loyalties and they turned on their masters. Grand scale undisciplined skirmishes exploded as these corrupt troops demanded taxes for their own use. The populace resisted, and squalls of massacres ensued. A civil war of sorts erupted with fractured alliances all around. Taking full advantage of this turn of events Karageorge first lead his comrades against the Janissaries, brilliantly gaining himself the full gratitude and appreciation of the Turks. Next he turned his troops and attention on them.

Karageorge's actions spoke for him. His courage and commitment were recognized by his brethren and they urged him to take the crown and become their king and leader. Karageorge refused to take any title, and I can only feel immense pleasure and pride that he was true to his word, that he was not looking for personal glorification. Instead, he was clearly on a mission to help himself and his people and he never lost sight of that. Just as important, he was perfectly aware of his explosive temperament and he openly warned his followers that while he might be a great warrior in times of conflict, he could never be counted on to be a peaceable leader and so he attempted to reject any such proposition. But after much remonstrating from his brothers in arms he eventually accepted and settled on the dignified but not outlandish title of Undisputed Leader. He had no interest in being a king, and that tells one so much about how he thought. It makes me like him all the more. He was dangerous, lethal even, but he was never a hypocrite. Here his legend truly blossoms and proliferates into his enduring dynasty, a pile-up of repeated exiles, executions, coronations and further assassinations for the next 200 or so years, right up until the present day, albeit in a softened civilized rendition. At least I hope so!

Belgrade, an ancient city, has had many iterations. In the early nineteenth century half of it was Turkish and Muslims controlled the impressive Kalemegdan Fort which today is part of a huge and beautiful park. One can stroll around and see the views of the Sava River, the Danube River and the island called Great War Island that sits between the land of Serbia and what was then the southern edge of Austria-Hungary and the wild swamp called the Military Frontier. South of this area, still a part of Belgrade, and now a purely residential and settled area of the capital city known as Vračar, was where Karageorge assembled his camp and a band of followers some 6,000 strong. A park here commemorates his exceptional victory with soft lawns of grass and dandelions and daisies and his enormous statue with his monstrous looking sword, and a small graveyard with time-worn headstones.

Contemporary Vračar is clustered with old and new buildings, from old slouching structures with slanting tiled roofs to modern cement blocks of condominiums, fronted with narrow sidewalks of sometimes crumbling stone. Here one must step carefully across busy streets of fast-moving cars, but on every corner is a traditional restaurant, each boasting the best Karageorge Schnitzel, a local tribute to the man; a combination of pork and chicken beaten into a slab of meat and then filled with kajmak – a local cheese – rolled up and deep fried. As if that was not enough, because the item looks vaguely unattractive, it is then slathered with tartar sauce and decorated with slices of tomato and lemon. One plate surely is enough to feed a village. The meal is delicious but near impossible to finish as it is intentionally and appropriately massive in honour of the hero. It is a matter of pride; a competition of sorts to see who can put away the most. On my first try I failed! In truth, however, I'm assured this was not a meal he ever ate and was instead invented by a crafty chef low on supplies when dignitaries stopped by his inn. So as to feed these unexpected guests the resourceful chef, using everything he could find in his kitchen storeroom, created what appeared to be a massive meal from almost random ingredients. I suggest fasting for several days before and after experimenting with this dish.

This area called Vračar, where Karageorge and his troops once lived and plotted and from where they made their successful assault on the enemy, is today very much a part of Belgrade. It is a bustling part of the metropolis, home to the Church of St Sava, one of the largest Orthodox churches in the world. Vračar is mostly residential and packed with restaurants and coffee houses, but in the days of Karageorge this would have been a forest. It was a good place from which to launch an attack and here he lived, with his formidable force of loyal followers prepared to die for their cause. By the spring of 1804, from as far away as the forests of Šumadija, he had 30,000 combat-ready men organized and prepared to strike in a widespread revolt. He led his troops against the Turks and until his conquest in 1806 this was a battleground, memorialized as the First Serbian Uprising. Using cannons, the firepower of the day and a Serbian zeal uniquely their own, they overwhelmed their enemies. Some say it was his brilliant military skill that earned Karageorge the recognition of Napoleon Bonaparte. Others will tell you this is a total fantasy. More likely it was the other way around and it was Karageorge who was inspired by the impressive legends of Napoleon's exploits.

~

A fragment from Karageorge's speech to the newly liberated Serbia:

> Therefore, dear Serb brothers… now when it's only up to us, take an example from those peoples who foster unity and order, for they have become mighty and prosperous; offer advice to each other, as the priests do, when they teach their flock; teach them the words of Christ, the ones which say: As I have loved you, so you also should love one another. Not so much by words, but by your deeds… by doing so, the end of our quest will bring out the old glory of Serbia to show who we indeed are: the children of our glorious and brave ancestors.
>
> The Proclamation of Karageorge
> in Liberated Belgrade (1809)

~

The Turks, long in the habit of managing unruly far-flung provinces by the use of force and stamping out any desires or hankerings for independence, capitulated to discussions with Karageorge. They despatched emissaries to convey their opinions and open a dialogue. Karageorge, however, summarily ignored them and declared himself Hereditary Supreme Leader of Serbia. Modern Serbia was born.

His triumphant liberation and rule would last until 1812. During these years he and Jelena had many children and he was hailed unequivocally as a hero. While Karageorge himself never left the country during these years, possibly so as to deter any threat of a coup, he did send representatives to Russia and Paris to communicate his standing and his central platform. This must have been an intoxicating time, a time of vindication for all that he had believed in and fought for. Equally important, however, with the French and the Russians at war, would have been his need to keep a close eye on foreign affairs. Sure enough, when Napoleon faltered in his Moscow campaign part of the net result was the Russians trading away Serbian protection in the Treaty of Bucharest.

Briefly, an element of these intricate negotiations included a stipulation which required the Serbs to lay down their weapons. Predictably, Karageorge defiantly refused and while, no doubt, his countrymen fully concurred they would all have known the repercussions this would ensure. As the Turks were now freed up from fighting Russia, the entire Ottoman armed forces were available to subdue Karageorge. With their full force they bore down on him and his intolerable defiance.

Serbs well understood the ramifications and that reprisals on a grand scale were heading their way. To his credit Miloš Obrenović held his ground and fought and while he survived the onslaught, many innocents were mowed down by the Turks who were intent on restoring order. On 21 September 1813 Karageorge, for the second time in his life, relocated his entire family to the Austrian Empire, out of harm's way. By the end of

1814 Jelena, the devoted wife of Karageorge, with all her children, had repaired to the relative safety of Sremska Mitrovica, a city located in the province of Vojvodina. Later, at the invitation of the tsar, she moved with her family to Russia.

With Karageorge temporarily out of the way, Miloš Obrenović went on to inspire the Second Serbian Uprising. But Obrenović was a different character altogether from the uncompromising Karageorge, and after two years of guerrilla warfare he restructured his ambitions and engaged directly with the enemy, allowing them effectively to persuade him toward a truce of sorts. This culminated in an oral agreement made on word of honour with the Ottomans, which included as one of many compromises the assurance of the extermination of the uncontrollable upstart Karageorge. In turn Miloš Obrenović could style himself a prince. One could argue this was in name only as he was always, ultimately, a subject of the Osmanli.

For more than a decade and a half, Jelena and her children lived in Chisinau (today the capital city of Moldova) and Hotin (then in Bessarabia and now in Chernivtsi Oblast of western Ukraine). Exile was emotionally difficult for her and for the first three years, while her husband was still alive, Jelena begged the Russian government – even directly petitioning the tsar – for permission to allow her and her family to return to Serbia. Rather creatively she offered this in exchange for Karageorge himself, the hunted man, to be sent to Russia in their place.

By 1817 Karageorge was in exile far away from his family and homeland. Where precisely is debatable. Some say he went to Austria-Hungary and then on to Greece, espying his homeland from the borders. Others insist he lived in Bessarabia enjoying the full protection of his Russian allies. Regardless of where he went, what is agreed upon is that he sincerely wished to return to his home at Topola, possibly if only to die. The ageing soldier sent word of his intentions to former comrade-in-arms Obrenović and in reply he was guaranteed safe passage. A clue to the trickery and false nature of this purported 'safe passage' was the obvious disrespect in the missive, when Obrenović referred to the great warrior as 'George Petrović', a slight Karageorge overlooked at his own peril.

It is likely that as a result of an arrangement with his over-lords, Prince Obrenović ordered the murder of Karageorge at Radovanjski Lug, when he had almost reached his home. Ambushed and decapitated, his head was despatched and pre-sented to the sultan in Constantinople. This assassination flagged the start of the Karageorgević-Obrenović feud which would end as bloodily as it began, just shy of 100 years later.

Years passed but Jelena and her family, despite having ample funds from the Russian government, were unhappy in their new home. Their hearts were broken and their desire to get home to Serbia intensified. Jelena was the first among them to accept that in Serbia Karageorge's time was gone forever, and that Miloš Obrenović was the acknowledged ruler.

She never gave up, and continually hoped to return to Serbia by reminding Prince Miloš that Karageorge was his godchild. Jelena sent a series of heartfelt letters to the ruling couple in Serbia reminding them of this honourable connection that she hoped would inspire leniency. Ljubica, the wife of Miloš, replied by letter in which she expressed great joy at the prospect of reuniting soon. However, her true feelings were made abundantly clear when she signed off not only as 'Godmother Ljubica M. Obrenović' but also, 'Princess of Serbia'. Still, Jelena

Petrović persevered with her intentions. The Russian tsar and the Serbian prince finally reached an agreement and in the spring of 1831 Jelena, along with her children, began the long journey home. At the same time multitudes of Serb refugees returned to their homeland. Unfortunately, at the beginning of that year Karageorge's widow and her youngest son Alexander, who was married to a prominent Serb and living in Bessarabia, had been issued Russian passports, meaning they were now stripped of their Serbian nationality.

The Russian government generously provided Jelena 1,000 ducats for travel costs, a significant amount at that time. In the summer of 1831 a caravan of Serb refugees arrived at the border and here began a fresh indignity. Border police officers ordered Jelena Petrović to return to Vlaska with her family and her entire retinue. For some reason they permitted entry only to Karageorge's daughter Stamenka and her own children. Meanwhile, Jelena was now trapped in a humiliating and hopeless position. Worse, she was no longer receiving her Russian stipend. Again, she contacted her 'dear Godfather' Obrenović and the Russian tsar, asking them if they really wished for her to 'live as a beggar', and if they would permit this lamentable state of affairs. Evidently, they would.

Meanwhile, Miloš's time on the Serbian throne was running out and in the summer of 1839 he was expelled from Serbia. In October 1839 Jelena at last arrived in Serbia after a full twenty-five years in exile. For her first two months back she gratefully received visits from the city's most prominent ladies and gentlemen, and the newspapers cautiously covered this news. Jelena, quite the shrewd diplomat by now, at once set about promoting her son Alexander who received a position in the Belgrade court.

Prince Mihailo, the son of Miloš, took Alexander as his aide. During the reign of Prince Mihailo, Jelena could do as she pleased. Jelena died in January 1842, aged seventy-five. Her last wish was to be buried beside her beloved Karageorge in Topola where she treasured her 'most beautiful memories'. Respectfully, Prince Mihailo led the funeral procession from Belgrade to Topola. A journalist of the *People's Journal* finished his article with the words, 'All of Serbia cried that day.'

Karageorge Petrović – liberator and founder of modern Serbia – was buried as a hero at the church of St George at Topola. To this day the town celebrates his memory with his image hung on every wall, from churches to private homes and coffee houses and bars. One hundred years after his death, his grandson King Peter I Karageorgević had him re-interred at the new family crypt, Oplenac, on a hill on the outskirts of the town of Topola. Today George Petrović – Karageorge – can be visited in this splendid mosaic and marble mausoleum, in a block of white rock with gold inscription. Two hundred years after his glorious liberation of the homeland, I left a white rose on his tomb and respectfully kissed the ice-cold stone.

As I examine 'Kara' George Petrović, I find an incontrovertible hero. I see a strong man of passion and righteous beliefs. I see someone who was driven to demand more than the status quo. He questioned the unnatural strictures of a foreign authority. He was not motivated by personal glory or shiny objects, and yet he would not sit idly by as his country strained for freedom. He was by nature a leader. I have briefly examined this history which to me becomes evermore fascinating the closer I stare. I did not know what I was looking for, and I did not know what I would find. The last thing I expected from this journey was to discover my own inner self reflected. Indisputably I feel great pride in his courage and daring against such enormous odds. Was he a savage, a noble savage or was he a warrior who fought for justice? You can decide for yourself. In my mind he did what came naturally to him in response to the times he lived in. But I ask you this: without him, what would Serbia be today?

5

HSH Prince Alexander I of Serbia

11 October 1806 – 3 May 1885

ALEXANDER KARAGEORGEVIĆ WAS BORN IN 1806 DURING the magnificent reign of his father Karageorge, the great hero. Alexander was the youngest of six children, but as is the way with Serbian heritage he was swiftly singled out as the chosen one who would inherit the title of prince and the rule of this newly-independent country of Serbia.

In direct contrast to standard procedure almost everywhere else where the eldest son is the first in line, Prince Alexander was groomed to rule, regardless of the fact that he was the youngest child of Karageorge and Jelena. This Prince Alexander was born in Topola at a time when his father was the leader of the country and all he would have known, in his early youth, was an unquestionable certainty of his position in life, his duty on Earth and most especially in Serbia. Alexander grew up with none of the typical concerns that afflict youngsters; he wanted for nothing, there was no issue of money or even ambition as his path in life was clearly set out before him. All that was expected of him was fairly simple: marry a princess or a noblewoman, learn the craft of warfare and governmental leadership, and stand up to foreign authority and any member of the Obrenović clan. At the same time he would have been fawned over by all those around him and treated like the dauphin he was led to believe he was. Pretty sweet childhood, even if it would turn out to be a gentle river before a treacherous cascading waterfall which no one could foresee. He was therefore designed for success, and this foundation would set him up with an inner strength and conviction that saw him through to the end of his days, regardless of the ever-changing landscapes in his life.

Where most modern people clamour for an answer to, 'What is the purpose of my life?' Prince Alexander would have uniquely been spared any such self-questioning, despite the deeply real fact that nothing was certain and quite soon the shifting quicksand beneath his feet would loosen. But belief in something is like meeting fate more than halfway, and can carry one along safely through the turbulence.

It goes without saying that one massive difference between this young prince and his father is that whereas Karageorge lived to fight against great odds and for the goal of freedom – and subsequently died for his beliefs – Alexander inherited a predetermined position along with a pension from the state and the admiration of his countrymen. Where, by stark contrast, his father was born a poor labourer who fought valiantly at a time when others were executed for such impetuosity and all that he earned he gained himself, Alexander reaped the rewards of his father's work. The differences of how these acts would shape a person are monumental and not to be overlooked. So while Karageorge had a sense of purpose, his son Prince Alexander would instead have had a sense of entitlement. That does not make his intentions bad, but it certainly alters them.

If rootlessness is the single most important element that debilitates a person, Prince Alexander, the dauphin if you like, benefitted from the exact opposite. What an extraordinary luxury. I imagine from my armchair-psychologist point of view this must have been a transformative situation that moulded his personality right from the start and encouraged and dictated his behaviour throughout his peculiar life. Were it not for his father's courage and determination, young Alexander might so easily have been born a farmer with a rake in his hand. Instead he fully expected to run a country.

Alexander's early childhood was a time of giddy glory because for the first ten years of his life his father was in charge of the country. This reality must have been heady and it would define his life's objective. I find this interesting because it proves how easily the human mind is conditioned and swayed by fantasy and fairy tales. This is not to say that his father's exploits were anything less than real and sensational but the influence they had on the minds of his children and later, their own descendants, supports the idea that all you need is to believe in something to make it a reality, at least in your own mind. Despite Alexander's father's ignoble end – a beheading no less – and the family's expulsion from their homeland, resulting in the next twenty-odd years living in Russia, and the meddling from powers abroad, Prince Alexander never thought of himself as anything but the natural successor to a country.

If you look at this with a cold eye you will agree, surely, that this is delusional, but such is the capacity of humans to believe and to hope and to thereby shape their own lives, to reach for that which is not theirs and yet convince themselves it is. I find this very interesting. Quite the opposite of a meritocracy, it is an assumption that can be lethally misleading to the extent that despite the changes on the world stage regarding the status of Serbia and Alexander's own individual position he never changed his mind about his own destiny. His mother, Jelena, would also have been responsible for encouraging this mentality as it was she who petitioned endlessly for the family's legal return to Serbia, and once back, it was due to her efforts her son was appointed to the ruling body of Mihail Obrenović. His fate was always clear to him and I am certain he never once questioned it. For sure, he never took a step back and thought of himself as a pig farmer who should till land and herd hogs. Such are the illusions man so swiftly constructs.

Following the protocol appropriate to the time, and to prepare him for his predetermined life as a leader of men, Prince Alexander was educated first at a boarding school in Geneva. He then continued his education at the Military School in St Petersburg, Russia. This showed the close ties between Russia and Serbia which played a role in the outbreak of World War I. This education in Russia was arranged by the tsar. Alexander attended the finest military academies and was instructed in the ways of soldiering. Keep in mind his own father, who wielded a sword half his own height and lugged cannons through the mountainous forests of Šumadija, never spent one day in such a military academy; he learned his craft on the battlefield. Which is the more reputable, I cannot say.

By the time Alexander was seven years old his father was despatched into permanent and disgraceful exile. Did this event lay a trail of doubt on his otherwise sure path? Obviously not.

I believe it should have if logic ever entered his mind. Instead it served to galvanize him and commit him all the more to his need and desire to return and rule.

At the pleasure of the tsar, young Prince Alexander stayed on in the Russian Empire, in an area then known as Bessarabia (now in the Ukraine). His mother and his siblings were soon to join him, also at the personal request and generosity of the tsar. They were provided with shelter and a pension, as was befitting their position and situation, according to the collective misunderstanding that they were of consequence at all. I do not say this disparagingly, but rather that, from my perspective, at this point they could have been let loose, merely another Serbian family. But already they were pawns and they, and everyone of influence around them, played their parts, granting themselves an importance that was entirely self-created and maintained at the bidding of those who would choose to use them. And why would they see themselves any differently, other than as the chosen and anointed ones? After all, they lived on stipends provided by the Russian government, arranged by the tsar himself. Alexander grew up with a firm belief in his sense of importance. So begins a dynasty.

~

A side note on the fickle nature of geographic borders: Moldova and Moldavia are the same. After becoming an independent country after the break-up of the Soviet Union, they insisted the name was Moldova, but before then in the West it was always called Moldavia. Most of eastern Moldova was part of the Russian

Empire as Bessarabia (and Hotin in northern Bessarabia, thanks to border changes at some point, is now in the Ukraine). After World War I Bessarabia became part of Romania. Then after World War II it was taken by the Soviet Union... and Moldova/ Moldavia was created as a Soviet Republic, which became independent in 1991. Got it? Me neither!

There were some Jewish families in Moldavia who had lived there for generations, for example, a particular family by the name of Oxenberg who worked modestly as tailors and butchers and who remained in this homeland until anti-Semitism breathed too strongly in their direction and they set sail for the new world. There exists the possibility Prince Alexander Karageorgević and an Oxenberg passed each other on a street corner in Bessarabia without any chance of recognizing any future significance. More than 100 years later the descendants of an Oxenberg and one of the Karageorgević clan would intertwine.

∾

Besides preparing himself as a soldier and a leader, Alexander stayed on in Russia, signing up with regiments and attending the best balls. Soon he turned his attention to finding a suitable bride, and on 20 May 1830 Alexander married Persida Nenadović, a beautiful girl from a prominent Serbian family also living in exile who had made a temporary home in Bessarabia. Already, Alexander knew that his life would be financially supported by the Russian ruling powers. The thought of earning his keep had been erased from his consciousness by virtue of his strange position as a ruler in waiting.

The young couple moved to an estate situated on the border with Romania, near a town named Temesvár (Temesvár being just one of many of a multitude of suggested spellings). All his life at Temesvár, Prince Alexander pined to get home to Serbia, unquestionably inspired and influenced by his father's legacy and his mother's very real and vocal determination. She would have told him the country was his to govern and he would have believed her.

Alexander and Persida first had a girl, Poleksija, in 1833; next Kleopatra in 1835; then Aleksije in 1836; and Svetozar in 1841. Finally their son Peter was born in 1844 and he was selected and anointed as their heir apparent. His younger brother Arsen and other siblings barely got a mention. As is the way in Serbia, while women were systematically passed over for succession, the critical factor was prowess. Peter was exactly who they were looking for. In Temesvár the children were home-schooled with tutors. For play, as much as training, there was hunting, shooting, fishing and riding – all useful skills no doubt.

It can be supposed that Prince Alexander lived a life of melancholy, maybe even wistfulness. As the son of the great leader Karageorge, he wholeheartedly believed in the elusive anticipation of his birthright – that Serbia was his country to rule. He had access to funds because Russia provided him an allowance, essentially supporting his understanding of his innately special status. He always expected it and diligently he waited in the border town until the opportunity presented itself. While he lived the life of an exile he was never morally defeated. Equally, it would have been unthinkable to him to simply walk away, to stroll off into a normal civilian life. Quite the opposite: he was at the ready so that when in 1842, at the request of the Serbian people, Prince Alexander was recalled to rule Serbia, he went post haste.

All his life his most fervent desire was to return to Serbia and assume his rightful position as leader. In 1842 his dreams came true and for sixteen years he ruled, and this was both a great time and a fraught time. He lived in splendour in an Austrian-inspired edifice in what is now central Belgrade, an impressive structure with pale yellow walls and tall windows topped with a gleaming spire crested by a massive gold eagle with widespread wings. His ambitions were to better the country, to modernize it as best he could.

Prince Alexander's consort Princess Persida Nenadović was more than merely a spouse and she involved herself in politics. No doubt with the best of intentions she encouraged her husband to surround himself with her brothers and her cousins for his closest cabinet members, ostensibly because they would be reliably loyal. Serbia has a male-centric mentality and this meddling by a woman might well have sped up his downfall. This action, though no doubt not the single cause of dissent, would be interpreted by the politicians of the day as an unwelcome usurping of power.

However, during Prince Alexander's reign it was generally accepted that he was a good ruler; a fair and even-handed monarch. He introduced important laws to the land and law courts were put in order, roads were built. Bringing new technologies invented in the West, he had telegraph poles erected, new mines opened and most importantly many schools and soldiers' academies were founded. Prince Alexander did this job with love and duty, and a sense of purpose, but all around Serbia Europe was an unholy mess in which he had no desire to involve himself or his people. With the majority of his attention on Slav-centric concerns, inevitable internal political strife curdled and the ancient feuding of local and neighbourly interests resulted in a morass of conflicts. Europe was modernizing itself with industrial revolutions and actual revolutions, and in America there was civil war. This newly forming land of States and its extraordinary experiment was forging ahead with its inventions and overturning of conventions. It was a time of equality for mankind (white men, to be specific) providing you overlook the issue of women's second-class citizenship. They were still not allowed the vote or even to manage money, and most egregiously there was the unforgivable matter of the ongoing slave trade.

Meanwhile, Prince Alexander kept his eye on local issues and helping his own homeland take the long overdue steps to carry it into more modern times. Unfortunately, the result of these internal conflicts – some would suggest they were encouraged by the meddlesome, self-serving desires of the powers abroad – was the restoration of the ageing Prince Obrenović. By 1858 Prince Alexander was pushed out and forced to return to his life as an exile. His short reign, while glorious, was over. His dutiful contribution had come and gone, yet in the eyes of the world it was barely a footnote. Prince Alexander was repeating the pattern of his father's life. He returned to the Romanian border town and settled the family, once again, at Temesvár.

A rumour – some would say it is more than a rumour – was that when Prince Alexander was expelled in 1858 he took with him a substantial amount of government funds. When he packed up to leave, he included in his suitcases the riches of Serbia's treasury. If this rumour has any merit, I think it is an important detail in illuminating the great difference between this Prince

Alexander and his own father, Karageorge, who no doubt would have been appalled and may even have gone so far as to mete out his own very special style of justice; for example, a shot in the head. Karageorge was never motivated by personal greed and he did not care for any form of self-aggrandizement, nor did he know avarice, so chances are if this rumour has any truth to it, he would not have tolerated it. On the plus side, this plunder allowed Prince Alexander and Princess Persida to live comfortably for the rest of their lives and to ably support their children.

Possibly Alexander would have tried to justify his actions, believing he was meant to be a king, and should live like one. His concerns were for himself and his family and with his freshly looted cash he returned to Temesvár and resumed life, except now he could fund his ambitions as never before. He had no thought of living as a private citizen, but rather as an exiled ruler, and he never relinquished his goal and commitment to returning. Following the tradition of the time and in the hopes of readying his offspring for their rightful inheritance, Prince Alexander sent the more robust of his children to be schooled in Paris and St Petersburg, preparing them for the next round of the dynastic feud.

His beloved wife Princess Persida died in 1873 and Prince Alexander was soon to follow in 1885 after living out the remainder of his life in Romania. Prince Alexander and Princess Persida would be buried side by side in Vienna. Just as in life, they were homeless in death, but they were not impoverished and their riches were passed on to their children. Their son and chosen heir Peter would carry the torch, just as they had hoped, and in 1912, as a crowned monarch, King Peter I would construct the family crypt. The bodies of the Karageorgević family were transferred to the newly-built mausoleum, Oplenac, at Topola. The family was united and the dynasty's legacy secured. The building itself is a magnificent jewel, and an appropriate resting place for people motivated to do good for their brethren, despite seemingly unscalable obstacles.

Peter fought bravely in both of the Balkan Wars, and World War I. He also appears to have inherited the gene for pomp and glory, which Karageorge did not have, but Peter's father Alexander displayed. Just look at the footage of Peter's coronation after his return from exile in 1904. Peter's younger brother Prince Arsen, in my opinion, garnered all of his grandfather's warring instincts and was a military man through and through. Also, just like his grandfather Karageorge, Arsen was not fit for peacetime. In fact, he had no interest whatsoever in any form of normal domestic life; his energies, which were not unsubstantial, were directed always toward fighting. If there is such a thing as a gene that dictates sadism, Arsen inherited more than his fair share. Arsen fought in wars as bravely as any samurai, with no concern for his own mortality, and when there was no war in which to engage, he endlessly challenged foes to duels.

Not to be overlooked, however, is the Europe of the nineteenth century which always used Serbia as a transit stop on the road to somewhere else. Foreigners endlessly manipulated strings and yet did not pay the country the least amount of sovereign respect. Consider the notations of an Englishman, Albany Fonblanque, which include his opinion of Prince Alexander as a 'weak' person. But how much credence should we grant this Englishman who, at the same time, in every letter home, whined relentlessly about his living arrangements, his very appointment and his wage. This Fonblanque is nevertheless important because he was the only Brit in the country despatching news at all, but his opinion is clouded with his misunderstandings of the people among whom he dwelt and his displeasure with being there at all.

Meanwhile, Prince Alexander conducted his life and thoughts according to his predetermined path, despite roiling Europe and its many intrigues spinning around like a cyclone. France exploded with revolution, Napoleon's nephew became bloated with anticipatory glory, Russia attempted to exert its influence on Palestine and Britain, or 'Great' Britain if you prefer, cosied up to the Ottomans, strictly for political purposes.

Montenegro, a tiny outpost on the Adriatic, flexed its claim for independence at a time when its own history was not even understood by those attempting to control it. I find it interesting that Serbia and Montenegro are the only countries in this region of the planet with royal families of their own blood, not transplanted and imposed Danes and Germans like all the others, stemming mostly from Britain's favourite German, Queen Victoria, and her far-reaching progeny who would populate the crowned heads of most of Europe. Victoria was not the first to do this. Catherine the Great of Russia, after all, was also of German origin.

The Crimean War, an enormous blight on the collective memories of Brits and Europeans alike, was a war about dominance over soil half a world away, and at the end of the bloodbath, after countless lives were lost, virtually nothing was changed, no ground gained. Some might argue it was utterly purposeless, unless you were the largest weapons manufacturers of the day, in which case you would have done extremely well.

Serbia was instructed by the British, rather stupendously, to side with their sworn enemy the Turks and at the same time to wage war against their single great ally, the Russians. This was merely for the purpose of military convenience. It overlooked the history of these players so completely as to convey a total ignorance or disregard of the past. Serbia, of course, refused this request, and its only choice was to declare neutrality, less from altruism and more from a very real sense of self-preservation.

Prince Alexander worked with Obrenović against the ludicrous demands of the Brits. Better the enemy you know, as they say. But what is most interesting to me is that while Europe raged and stamped about hoping to redraw borders for their own benefit, and posturing wildly as they went, Prince Alexander and little Serbia ticked along, almost untouched by this worldwide aggression.

You can read despatches from British diplomats, mostly based in Cairo and making occasional visits to the Balkans, attempting to analyse the local situation, looking always to substantiate their own needs and claims – and yet Prince Alexander and Serbia are barely mentioned at all, even though he was a central figure of consequence. Perspective is a multifaceted thing of tremendous importance.

6

HRH Prince Arsen of Yugoslavia

16/17 April 1859 – 19 October 1938

Prince Arsen, the youngest son of Prince Alexander I of Serbia and Princess Persida, was a member of the House of Karageorgević and forebear of the current junior branch of the Yugoslav royal family. Arsen's only child was my grandfather Prince Paul. He was the grandfather of my mother, Princess Elizabeth of Yugoslavia, and my great-grandfather. Prince Arsen was a lethal beast fully invested with the ferocity of his fabled grandfather Karageorge and yet during his lifetime this savagery would become an anachronism, almost an embarrassment. Was this savage gene inherited from his grandfather?

While his actions as a warrior were rewarded with rows of medals, his ferocity was as legendary as it was outlandish and for his excesses he would one day be officially banished from his homeland. He was neither born in, nor ever lived in, this homeland, yet he was officially not permitted to be there, not even to fight in their army. What would Karageorge have made of this, I wonder?

Prince Arsen was the bravest of warriors and it is too bad for him he lived at a time when civility was prized over bloodshed. Compared to his own fiery temperament, Serbia, at least diplomatically, had been tamed, forcing him to sign up for wars elsewhere. His barbarity was out of proportion with the times in which he lived. I can't help feeling his grandfather would have favoured him and his boundless courage.

Prince Arsen was the youngest grandson of Karageorge, and yet he seems to be the closest to his great ancestor in terms of his warlike temperament. What is dissimilar is that although Karageorge was best known and appreciated for his valour, he also appears to have bonded with his children and been devoted to his wife Jelena. Prince Arsen, on the other hand, seems only to have inherited the gene for warfare.

Arsen, the very last child of Alexander and Persida, was born at Temesvár, Romania in 1859 – just one year after his father had been dislodged from the Serbian throne. Arsen was one of nine children. And while he, along with his older brother Peter, was groomed for the much-anticipated return to the homeland, his position in second place made him more of a spare than an heir. This in no way diminished his fervour. He grew up feasting on stories of the glory of Karageorge and he watched his own older brother, Peter, earn a reputation for heroics; first as a volunteer in the final stages of the Franco-Prussian War and later as a *hajduk* rebel fighting back in the homeland. These exploits must surely have inspired Arsen who was still too young to join in. Later, at the personal request of the ruling Obrenović prince, young Prince Peter was banished from Serbian territory where he was fighting for Obrenović. Perhaps it was because Obrenović feared that the popularity of a Karageorgević would unseat his reign; that young

Arsen was swollen with pride and all the more determined to earn his stripes as the greatest warrior of his day. While Prince Peter left Serbia a hero, in later years, after displaying too great a thirst for bloodshed, Prince Arsen was officially banned from the country at a time when the Karageorgević family were back on the throne. What a strange fate for the grandson of the mighty warrior Karageorge.

With the obvious limitations of life in rural Romania, Arsen was sent to be educated at prestigious schools in Paris, just like his brother Peter, and at the best military academy in St Petersburg. While Peter was groomed for succession, Arsen's role was less specific. Itching to exercise his fighting skills after so many years of training at the military academy, and still living in Russia, all Arsen could do to slake this bloodthirstiness was attend the most brilliant of parties, get very drunk and challenge foes to duels over slights big and small. Prince Arsen was by now a fixture in St Petersburg; with his military schooling completed and keen to demonstrate his abilities, he engaged in duels where he developed a penchant for shooting his opponents in the groin. Here is one account by Petar Ćuković from *The Court of King Nikola*: 'At a ball in St Petersburg in 1890, a quarrel broke out between two noblemen over a dance partner (Princess Elena of Montenegro, the future Queen of Italy)… which culminated in a duel… Prince Arsen of Serbia wounded Baron Mannerheim (future regent and commander-in-chief of Finland)…'

Not only does Princess Elena – born Princess of Montenegro who would go on to marry the future King of Italy – return as a figure of tremendous importance many years later in the life of my grandfather Paul, of equal interest is that in the diaries of Baron Carl Gustaf Mannerheim there is no mention of this duel with his 'great friend' Prince Arsen. But proof exists, in a verse penned by Ludwig Petzl, a poet of the Viennese court, who wittily and lightly refers to the battle between the prince and the baron. Translated from the original German:

Skilful Russians

> Once they shared a table and raised glasses of hope.
> Now they grasp at each other's hangman's rope.
> Lamentable, inconsolable woe.
> Divided by deadly slander today,
> They prepare to dig one another's graves.
> Why does not the colonel, in his disgrace,
> Laugh in ruthless Arsen's face before
> His likely departure to an eternal resting place?
> Hark, the time of judgement has struck,
> Pick your pistol, 'tis already cold, you're out of luck.

Prince Arsen's life in Russia was impressive and splendid, but this interested him less than pulling out a pistol and killing an enemy. He attended the best dances in the grandest houses as he was close friends with the tsar and the rest of the imperial Romanov family. Prince Arsen was a known quantity on the Russian social scene. He was after all, despite his legendary hot temper and love of duels, a prince, so when he was personally introduced to his future wife by the tsar he accepted his fate.

This union was essentially an arranged marriage between himself and a young Demidoff heiress, worth a fortune on a par with the tsar. On 1 May 1892 in St Petersburg, Arsen married Princess and Countess Aurora Pavlovna Demidoff di San

Donato. For the first few months the couple were blissfully happy, settled in St Petersburg, and Arsen and Aurora promptly sired one son and heir, my grandfather Paul. But Prince Arsen swiftly abandoned his vows and left for the front lines; he would never marry again. He was quite simply designed for warfare not romance.

Meanwhile, after handing over baby Paul to her brother-in-law Peter, who was by then living in Geneva, Princess Aurora relocated to Italy. Here she soon remarried and went on to have more children. I believe my grandfather had no relationship with these half-siblings, except for one half-brother who showed up many years later at his townhouse on the rue Scheffer. In the large sitting room on the second floor, the half-brothers, meeting for the first time in their lives, chatted politely for half an hour. My grandfather's version was that this half-brother greeted him and addressed him correctly (all very formal and according to protocol) and then they never saw each other again.

Some say Princess Aurora and Prince Arsen were unsuited, but evidently there was some common ground. They both had respectable titles, they had good health, good looks and great fortunes of their own. Very soon Princess Aurora and Prince Arsen lost touch, first with each other and subsequently with their only child Paul whom no one wanted to care for.

Arsen and his son Paul had the flimsiest of relationships but they knew each other, and they were civil. Perhaps one should say their relationship befitted the times and circumstances. That my grandfather did not experience any sort of idyllic childhood can be put into context, and while heartbreaking, it can be understood. My grandfather was essentially orphaned and then passed around to reluctant relatives, and all this sounds a bit tragic, except that, luckily for him, he was emotionally taken care of by various angels along the way.

In 1904, Paul was already living in Serbia with his uncle Peter and, to celebrate the return of the Karageorgević dynasty, Prince Arsen was also in Belgrade, plausibly to make himself available as muscle. His little son was there but Prince Arsen had not come to babysit; he was there to take charge of a country in a state of high alert. His ten-year-old son, Paul, was not really a big part of anyone's plans, and his life went on around him.

Prince Arsen threw himself into the fray of the newly-restored country. However, evidently he showed far too much in the way of muscle and his behaviour got him formally banned from Serbia. He moved back to Russia and stayed there until the Bolsheviks took over when there was no more room for royals of any nationality. Prince Arsen lived to fight; it was in his blood which he inherited directly from Karageorge. He fought in wars all over the world. His experience was a life of military duty in which he excelled. His training and skills perfectly suited his nature, and for his efforts he would become an admired and decorated soldier. At any other time he might have been marginalized as a psychopath and warehoused.

Prince Arsen was a wildly courageous fighter who felt keenly enough to repeatedly risk his own life in daring feats of valour. He fought for the French Foreign Legion in Algeria, he fought on the front line in Vietnam, and for his exploits he received the *Légion d'honneur*. He further distinguished himself in the Balkan Wars of 1912 and 1913. The Serbian army took note of his methods and apparently he showed himself as a savage of such unparalleled proportions that when World War I began the Serbian army refused him a position.

Instead, he made his way to Russia – offering his services – where he was made a General of the Horse Guards. Here he excelled, if your measure of excellence is enemy casualties. Finally, this was the right time and the right place for all he had to offer, and his prowess was gratefully recognized. But with the looming inevitable changes in ideology, and as a close ally of the tsar, it would become imperative that he leave the country or risk losing his life. This intractable inevitability made itself overtly apparent when he was arrested by the Bolsheviks at the start of the Russian Revolution. He was rescued by the intervention of a French ambassador, whereupon he concealed himself in a sealed wagon and escaped. Neither Prince Arsen – nor any royal – was welcome in Bolshevik Russia.

With his public and formal banishment from Serbia his options were limited, but I doubt he felt aggrieved by this. If anything he quite likely felt pride at being considered such a danger. Whatever his feelings about this he chose to settle in Paris where he threw himself into a life of wine, women and gambling just as thoroughly as he had into the wars in which he fought. Prince Arsen's life in Paris is well documented and while he had no one left to fight, he did not curtail his rambunctious habits. He became legendary as a reckless gambler, a rampant womanizer and something of a drunk. His reputation so exceeded the norm that a Parisian barmaid refused his proposal of marriage. With the rest of the Karageorgević family installed in Serbia, Prince Arsen was officially banned from the country. No doubt he took this as a huge compliment.

However, this ban seems to have been somewhat lax as I continually come across photographs of my great-grandfather in Serbia during these years. In one such photograph he is seated at afternoon tea on an outdoor terrace with King Alexander and Queen Maria. In defiance of the ban he is clearly there, and interestingly sometimes he is dressed in civilian clothes despite his military predisposition. Equally, there are photographs of him in uniform bedecked with a solid row of gleaming medals of honours earned in battle. It was enough metal to weigh down the shoulders of a weaker man, but he was no weakling and he stands tall and proud and very serious in these black-and-white shots.

Arsen lived long enough to span the turn of the century, to see the very name of his fatherland change from Serbia to Yugoslavia, to witness his dynasty restored to the monarchy. It was a country where he was not welcome, and I have to wonder how that felt. Then, right in front of his ageing eyes, Yugoslavia was handed to his son Paul, his only child, a relative stranger to him. How did he feel about this, regardless of the estrangement, when his own son was chosen over him?

In the photograph that exists of Arsen in Belgrade in 1934, you see him walking in the sombre procession of the funeral after the assassination of King Alexander I, the loved and feared leader. Prince Arsen looks deadly serious and deeply complex, and evidently and awkwardly apart from the others. In the forefront is the young future King Peter, still a child and visibly bewildered, clinging to his mother the widow Queen Maria. The Queen and Princess Olga (Prince Paul's wife, my grandmother) walk side by side, in traditional mourning regalia of long, layered black gowns reaching to their ankles and elaborate veils of black lace – like Spanish mantillas – covering their heads and faces. King Carol of Romania is speaking closely into the ear of my grandfather Prince Paul, who was suddenly created regent.

All the men wear heavy coats with ceremonial belts and sashes and medals and stars. They wear black armbands on the sleeves of their overcoats. My grandfather has his cap held in a white-gloved hand, clutched by the brim with its gold insignia, his face deadly serious.

Arsen and his son Paul do not look at each other and keep far apart, in separate worlds. What was Arsen thinking? Was he feeling outraged at having been passed over in succession? Did Prince Paul even for the merest moment contemplate offering this regency to his father? Did they consider each other at all beyond their duty to be civil and get it all over and done with? I can only speculate. When Arsen lay dying in Paris, I wonder if he thought analytically over the choices of his life. He had lived to fight, but what had he been fighting for? By chance, in the autumn of 1938, my grandmother Princess Olga was in Paris. It was a sad time for Olga who lost her adored father when he died in Athens at the beginning of that year. She was in Paris visiting her Greek and Romanov relatives, many of these royals being in a suspended state of relocation due to repeated exile. By then many had put down tentative roots elsewhere, if not permanently, then certainly to wait and see what the future had in store for them.

During my grandmother Olga's Parisian sojourn tragedy continued to strike: her uncle, Grand Duke Kirill Vladimirovich of Russia, died at Neuilly near Paris on 12 October 1938. I suppose one can be grateful he died of natural causes after so many relatives had lost their lives unnaturally early and in a grisly manner. Along with family members, Olga soon departed from Paris for Rosenau Castle near Coburg, Germany to attend the funeral.

Perhaps because of her close relationship with her own family she had a soft spot for her husband's father, the unique Arsen, and she took the time to stop by and visit her father-in-law. In a letter to my grandfather, Olga mentions that Arsen was lying in his bed in a terribly weakened condition, the room in disorder. Prince Arsen's later years had been entirely dedicated to a dissolute existence and he drank and gambled and whored his way through what money he had. His son Paul, for whom he had never given a moment's thought, made arrangements for his reckless father to receive a monthly allowance and in my grandmother's letter she mentions she noticed the most recently sent cheques were not only uncashed but strewn about the floor of his messy room. Arsen lay coughing and ill on his bed, too weak to speak.

On 19 October 1938, seven days after Olga's visit, HRH Prince Arsen of Yugoslavia died alone in Paris. It is quite likely my grandmother was the last visitor he received at his shamefully squalid home. Arsen's earthly remains were entombed at the family crypt, Oplenac, where, at last, after a lifetime in exile, he rests in Serbia.

Prince Arsen was a decorated warrior, and no doubt a lousy father. He seems to be the carrier of the harshest of Karageorge's genes. He lived to fight and he fought brilliantly. He was not unkind to his son, he was simply otherwise preoccupied. He was not intentionally cruel when he abandoned his single, lonely, frightened child, despite coming from a fairly normal and loving family himself. He just did not have it in him. What he did have was the fighting gene, and he pursued that natural inclination as far as he could.

I do remember my uncle Alexander, my mother's older brother, often laughingly retelling the story of how Prince Arsen was a very good shot, and when he aimed his pistols at his opponents in those frequent duels, he hit his enemy where it hurt the most: in their pride and joy. Beyond that, Prince Arsen was never discussed. I understand he was not of much interest to my grandfather who was a gentle soul, and who would have been disappointed on a deeply fundamental level by his utterly distracted father.

Prince Arsen was brought up in a loving environment, and his son Paul also cared for his own three children with love and care and a hands-on approach. For whatever reason, Arsen himself was incapable of delivering succour as he had received it. Perhaps these strange traits are recessive and show up randomly. Neither Darwin nor the best of today's geneticists can agree on much, so I do not expect to sort out here and now why Arsen was how he was. All I can say is that while one would not wish to be his offspring, no doubt his own grandfather would have felt nothing but pride for him. I feel compassion for my grandfather but such are the vagaries and ironies of the human condition.

I am certain Karageorge would have been fiercely gratified by his youngest grandson who formed his own opinions about how to live his life, and put that life on the line repeatedly in the name of courage and indomitable fearlessness. Does this mean Prince Arsen had a touch of the family sadism? Perhaps. But it is the same trait that brought him personal satisfaction and public acclaim.

My grandfather never talked about Arsen, his own father, but then again, he did not talk about his mother either. He kept a poker face as much to the world as to himself and when I think about it, I realize this may have been a coping mechanism. Without a doubt, Prince Arsen failed epically as a father, giving no attention at all to his only offspring. However, I believe Karageorge would have forgiven him even this because Prince Arsen's beliefs were honourable and rock solid. Arsen believed in strength, in courage and in winning, and when you accept that he was breastfed on such tales of his grandfather's celebrity, perhaps that explains him the best.

7

Princess and Countess Aurora Demidoff di San Donato

2/3 November 1873 – 28 June 1904

AURORA, MY GRANDFATHER'S MOTHER, WAS SURELY A romantic. She was beautiful in a doll-like way with her pale skin and melancholy, large, dark eyes. Ruled by her instincts for love, it appears she followed her heart. This included dalliances and romances with paramours while she was still married to her first husband, the incorrigible Prince Arsen of Serbia. It was shocking behaviour at the best of times. She was of the rarefied, sheltered, moneyed class and the cause of her greatest ennui would have been hunting for a suitable mate, or better yet a soulmate. Her heart took her on journeys in and out of liaisons, quite unseemly for a young lady of her stature at any time.

If you look her up online – as I did because my family seems to know very little – you will read that Aurora was a Russian noblewoman of the Demidoff family. She was the daughter of Pavel Pavlovich Demidoff, second Prince of San Donato, and his second wife Princess Elena Petrovna Trubetskaya. Aurora's paternal grandparents were the Swedish-Finnish philanthropist Aurora Stjernvall Karamzin and her Russian husband Pavel Nikolaievich Demidoff. This begs the question, who are these Russian Finns with their Italian titles, Napoleonic connections, mammoth wealth, and aristocratic wives?

Since the middle of the eighteenth century the Demidoff family were considered influential Russian merchants, industrialists and some would even call them a noble family. By the late eighteenth and early nineteenth centuries the Demidoff fortune was second only to that of the tsar himself.

Things were not always so. In the late seventeenth century Nikita Demidoff was a common serf, toiling as a blacksmith in Tula, a town 100 or so miles south of Moscow. In 1694, while Nikita was methodically pounding the heavy hammer on his anvil, a carriage emblazoned with the imperial arms pulled up outside. A steward hurried over to Nikita and asked him to repair a pistol which had jammed. Nikita agreed and, as he was going about his work, he heard a voice from inside the carriage lament the necessity to send abroad for beautiful and reliable firearms. Nikita, as he worked to unjam the pistol, laughed loudly and impetuously answered back that such weapons were easy to make. Like a vision from heaven, the man who stepped out of the carriage was no less than the tsar, Peter the Great. Nikita would have bowed but before he had the chance, the tsar took his calf-skin gloves and slashed the boastful blacksmith across the face.

Nikita touched his cheek, feeling the burn on his skin from the slap of those soft leather gloves, and ran off to his workshop. He knew exactly what to do and he fetched a pair of pistols equal, or superior, to the one he had been handed for repair. Peter the Great was mesmerized by what he saw and the two men, lovers of fine weaponry, settled easily into a position of mutual respect. The tsar invited Nikita to lunch at the palace. After Nikita left the palace his life was changed forever. Not only had he been granted his freedom, he was also deeded precious lands in the Urals – lands rich in iron ore, copper, silver and gold.

This single occasion had the lasting effect of not only changing Nikita's life, but changing the lives of his descendants some several hundred years later, including those of the Demidoff family members of the present day who live comfortably, I'm told, in Finland; and others elsewhere who now go by the name of Tissot.

Nikita turned this extraordinary stroke of luck into an enduring and profitable business. With his skill as a manufacturer of weapons and his understanding of the rules of business he established an iron foundry in Tula, dedicating himself as the tsar's personal munitions maker. During Russia's many wars the Demidoff factory in Tula worked prodigiously, maintaining a vital level of production for the government, perhaps directly affecting the outcome of these wars. In return Nikita Demidoff, the former serf, garnered a monumental income. In 1720, Peter the Great, with whom he was a personal favourite, ennobled him.

The status of nobility was made hereditary in 1726. However, while the Demidoff's wealth was solid, their position in Russian society remained 'nouveau'. Therefore, when great-grandson Nicholas Demidoff married Baroness Elisabeth Alexandrovna Stroganoff it was considered a prominent step up in society. Nevertheless, to avoid the elitist prejudices of St Petersburg, Nicholas Demidoff and his bride moved to France. Napoleonic Paris was a place of refinement, elegance and opulence if you could afford it. The Demidoffs certainly could and they thrived.

With magnificent wealth, a Russian noble status and a flair for international society, they set the stage for the later achievements of their eldest son, Anatole.

Anatole Demidoff was to carry his parents' social, literary and artistic ambitions to fulfilment. He was the corporeal fusion of a passion for the arts and all the sensitivities that implies, along with the pharaonic wealth to realize his most fantastic dreams. Though he had no children of his own he is a critical link to his descendants; he would bequeath magnificent treasures to them, not least the newly-created title of Prince of San Donato bestowed upon him by the Grand Duke of Tuscany in an attempt to elevate Anatole's status and retool him as a prize for Napoleon's niece Mathilde.

Anatole was raised in the impressive villa of San Donato which his father built north of Florence. He was cultured, charming and handsome and, perhaps predictably, made a spectacular marriage to Napoleon's formidable niece, Princess Mathilde Bonaparte, who happened also to be a cousin of the tsar and the future Napoleon III. Her credentials were impeccable while his endowment was beyond reproach. Mathilde was the daughter of Napoleon's brother Jérôme, who was always notoriously short on cash. Meanwhile, Anatole – who was one of the greatest art collectors of his time – knew many things, but he could not read a woman. He mistook Mathilde for a naive and easy lass. She was anything but that. Mathilde was a modern lady, independent and emancipated, and the instant they married she revealed her indomitable and imperious ways.

They were both headstrong and stubborn. The marriage was over before it had begun. It is possible the marriage was in trouble before the rings were slipped on each other's fingers.

Mathilde's impoverished father and Anatole had been engaged in a protracted negotiation over the dowry and the prenuptial agreement was heatedly tussled over.

As a result of his wife's close blood relationship with her uncle Napoleon – and her imperial Russian connections – Anatole was awarded the newly-fashioned title of Prince of San Donato. The marriage, celebrated on 3 November 1840, would not last. The story of Anatole and Mathilde may have begun as a fairy tale but it soon went horribly wrong. It is possible that in the beginning they married for love. They shared a knowledgeable and passionate interest in art and Anatole's collections of Dutch Masters and the Romantic artists expanded with the influence of Mathilde. However, her father Jérôme's inability to honour his obligation towards the payment of the dowry infuriated Anatole, especially because Jérôme repeatedly asked for money. Mathilde's father, for the last time, tapped Anatole and the marriage was dealt an irreversible blow. Instead of separating, first they took to parrying their rage with public humiliations. Mathilde used the French press to demolish Anatole's previously reproachless character. In this battle she was surely the victor, but battles, as we know, do not a war win.

First Anatole, and then Mathilde, took up with others, making no effort to disguise their love affairs and seemingly enjoying the indignity they heaped upon each other until finally only a divorce would do. The divorce proceedings were as ugly as any modern public split, with Anatole vigorously and relentlessly pursuing an open legal challenge against Mathilde to return his property, including a famous cache of enormous diamonds, and the restitution of the dowry. Mathilde's response was a series of cruel and personal attacks launched without subtlety via the media. Anatole's diamonds were never returned to him and his reputation was never recovered.

Mathilde moved back to Paris while Anatole lived on at San Donato writing a series of travel books (such as *Travels in Southern Russia, and the Crimea; through Hungary, Wallachia & Moldavia, during the Year 1837*), which would become respected works. He also collected paintings and furniture with which to enhance the beauty of his homes. While Anatole's life was sumptuous beyond imagination, and his time was devoted to acquiring evermore splendid objects, sadly his magnificent marriage had irretrievably faltered and he produced no heirs. When Anatole died, much of his precious collection was auctioned and thereby forever dispersed. Even the Villa San Donato was considered too closely associated with sad memories and sold.

Meanwhile in Finland, the young Eva Aurora Charlotte Stjernvall was born on 1 August 1808. Aurora was from a respectable Finnish-Swedish family. Aurora was appointed as a lady-in-waiting to Empress Alexandra Feodorovna the elder (consort to Tsar Nicholas I of Russia), and later in life a Lady of the Bedchamber to Empress Maria Feodorovna (wife of Alexander III) and Empress Alexandra Feodorovna the younger (wife of Nicholas II). She was made a Dame of the Order of Saint Catherine, the highest honour for ladies in imperial Russia.

In 1836 she married Anatole's younger brother Pavel Nikolaievich Demidoff (1798–1840). In 1846, after Demidoff's death, she married Andrei Karamzin. After the death of Aurora's second husband, she withdrew from romantic pursuits and instead occupied herself with the practical matters of her manor in Finland, and with her growing interest in charity. Aurora Karamzin used the immense wealth inherited from her first husband to create benevolent institutions in Helsinki such as schools, public kitchens and the Deaconess Institution of Helsinki. She was considered a great benefactor in many cities such as St Petersburg and Florence.

Pavel Nikolaievich and Aurora's only child was Pavel Pavlovich Demidoff (1839–85). In 1870 Pavel Pavlovich succeeded his childless uncle, Anatole Demidoff, as the second Prince of San Donato. Anatole's estate was extensive, including the princely title and all of this passed to his nephew. Just one small portion of this inheritance was the Villa Demidoff, near Florence outside the town of Prato.

The original and immensely grand Villa Reale was built by a Grand Duke of Tuscany in 1581, supposedly to impress his mistress. By the eighteenth century the estate was deserted. In 1820 Grand Duke Ferdinand III decided to demolish the villa with the help of explosives, and redesigned the garden. Luckily he left intact a large building known as the Paggeria which, in 1830, was sold to Anatole Demidoff who restored the Paggeria and named it the Villa Demidoff di Pratolino.

Nephew Pavel Pavlovich, who would inherit this magnificence, spent many happy years of his life here and even died there. The villa was a world of its own with its famously beautiful ornate park and orchards and statuary and fountains and lakes and follies, not to mention Giambologna's statue the *Appennino*, a statue I played in as a child. My grandfather, the grandson of Pavel Pavlovich Demidoff, was lucky enough to inherit Villa Demidoff. My favourite cousin HRH Prince Dimitri of Yugoslavia and I have many happy memories of this magical place. Our childhood led us to believe in fairy tales because to us they were real and they were tangible, unlike stories of Santa or even

Dracula; we saw and felt and tasted and lived in these fairy tales, so while I know intellectually this world of pomp and ceremony is gone forever, in my heart a large part of me still resides there. It was a time so formal and so different from today, a time when I curtsied and kissed my grandparents' hands every time we said hello or good morning or good night, and in turn they would make the sign of the Orthodox cross on my forehead. Can you imagine the shock when I came to America and saw children cursing their own parents?

While Pavel Pavlovich was still merely Count Pavel Pavlovich Demidoff, he made a first marriage in 1867 to Princess Maria Elimovna Meshcherskaya. She died two days after giving birth to a son, Elim Pavlovich Demidoff, third Prince of San Donato. The loss of his wife had a lasting effect on Pavel, who remained inconsolable for an extended spell.

In St Petersburg in 1871 he married the Princess Elena Petrovna Trubetskaya with whom he had six children: Nikita, Aurora, Anatoly, Maria, Pavel and lastly Elena, all of them taking the title count and prince or countess and princess, making themselves valuable marriage commodities. Unlike the worldly Anatole in his palaces stuffed with only the absolute best of the best paintings and priceless objects, nephew Pavel and his wife Elena lived in St Petersburg, a city considered more cosmopolitan than Moscow. Yet the heart of civilization, in those days, was Paris and Rome and, to a degree, London. Apart from the lives of the imperial family, Russia was considered mostly an unruly backwater.

While Elim became a Russian diplomat and eventually settled in Greece, his sister Maria – known inside the family as Moina – made a spectacular marriage to Prince Semyon Semyonovich

Abamelek-Lazarev. Moina's husband was a famous and cultured Russian traveller with whom she lived in a palatial villa in Rome. This Villa Abamelek was bequeathed to my grandfather Paul by Moina when she died in the 1950s. She also left him a stash of priceless jewels, including a famously fabulous Boucheron tiara my grandmother Olga wears in a photograph shot by Cecil Beaton. The Villa Abamelek was as ornate as the Vatican. In the redistribution after World War II the Soviets made this villa, with all its contents, their embassy. My grandfather Paul tried to sue for the return of his property, but he was unsuccessful.

When I say Aurora's experience of the world was like living inside a pearl, this was a pearl of sumptuousness on a level which can dazzle a covetous human, but it did not guarantee happiness. While Russia was already smouldering, Aurora lived inside the pearl, untouched by political events. She was born into the very fantasy modern girls dream of. She was born a princess; she was beautiful; she was abundantly wealthy; she was surrounded by priceless, beautiful objects with which to enhance her life. I wonder if she ever acknowledged any of this, if she ever understood in her heart how many blessings were bestowed on her at birth, but I doubt it, because it is the human condition to always want what you do not have. It appears, from her pursuits, all she craved was romantic love.

With the encouragement and blessing of Tsar Alexander III she married a far older, yet appropriate, candidate: Prince Arsen of Serbia, of the House of Karageorgević, a decorated and much-admired soldier already well known for his valour, among other traits. On paper at least she got it right. Less than a year after the wedding nuptials, Aurora gave birth to a son and heir. They named him Paul after her own father. Her father, Pavel

Pavlovich, was a Demidoff and it was through him that they had inherited the superb wealth and princely title which padded their lives. In theory everything was perfect. She had it all, and yet she was, it appears, restless and unsatisfied. The gullible romantic nineteen-year-old thought she had done well in her wedding to Arsen Karageorgević, Prince of Serbia, in St Petersburg on 1 May 1892. They produced a son, Paul, and yet, even before this birth the marriage was in tatters. Arsen wore out his wife with jealous accusations while all Aurora wanted was love.

The story goes that Aurora filed for divorce from Arsen and was granted her freedom in 1896. A story circulates – though it's hard to find firm facts on this issue – there was also a set of twins born in 1896 who were not recognized by Arsen as his, but nonetheless they had the legal name of Karageorgević because Aurora was still married while she was pregnant. The twins were called Alexandra and Nicholas. Rumours suggest Nicholas died of a drug overdose in the early 1930s. A sad start and a sadder end.

Aurora gamely moved on with her life and married Count Nicola di Noghera in 1897 with whom she had more children. Aurora probably never understood herself, let alone her husbands, and certainly not her children. Whether she was even interested in anyone beyond herself is hard to establish. She lived and died inside that mysterious pearl we call good fortune, without any possibility of knowing her distinct experience would very soon face extinction by firing squad. Her harshest brush with reality was the time she was left to care for her first baby, Prince Paul. When he was still a tiny baby Aurora wasted no effort begging family members to adopt her boy. She asked her older half-brother Elim, but he declined for professional reasons. Aurora asked everyone and anyone to take the child.

We do not know exactly how many children Aurora had. In the case of my grandfather, her first child, she could barely wait to get rid of him; after months of shopping him around she did finally get a taker in the form of her brother-in-law Peter, Arsen's older brother, then living a lonely life in exile in Geneva, his wife already dead and his children sent off to boarding schools. Peter agreed to take in his nephew who was sent, along with his Russian nurse, to his new home in Switzerland.

Princess Elena of Montenegro was the sister of King Peter's late wife Zorka, and therefore an aunt to Paul's cousins. Elena would marry the future King of Italy. It was over Elena that Paul's father, Arsen, had fought one of his many duels, which may have been one of a multitude of reasons she developed a tender attachment to the orphaned Paul when she first became acquainted with him in Geneva, all of eighteen months old and persistently asking after his mother. Elena felt a tenderness for the frightened child, and informally adopted him. She would become one of those many angels who appeared in his life, balancing out the grotesque emotional and very real abandonment to which he was repeatedly subjected.

Meanwhile, Paul's biological mother, Aurora, died in Turin in 1904. She never knew that her death coincided with the end of an age of decadence and dissolute behaviour, to which she formidably, though obliviously, contributed.

HM King Peter I of the Serbs, Croats and Slovenes

29 June 1844 – 16 August 1921

'My grandfather (Kara George) was a peasant, and I am prouder of that than of my throne. Crowns are lost, but the pure clean blood of those who have lived of the earth does not die.'

King Peter I quoted in *The History of Serbia*
Harold W. V. Temperley

As a grandson of the great Karageorge, Prince Peter's life would become the manifestation and fulfilment of any dynasty founder's goals. Peter's life ambitions were never certain and he would spend his days on the sidelines, waiting patiently and finally attaining the greatest trophy of all. He would be invited back to the country after nearly an entire lifetime in exile and be crowned king. He took this all very seriously, and he would go on to be loved and respected by the people of Serbia and to this day he is considered nearly as much of a hero as Karageorge.

Peter was the older brother of Arsen, my great-grandfather, and so for me Peter is a close emotional tie to this distant trip down the lane of history. Just as importantly to me, it was Peter who informally adopted my grandfather and gave him a home when no one else would. Peter is therefore important to me on a personal and intimate level, and it is with pleasure that I see he means so much to the people of Serbia. To the country he remains steadfastly a hero who waited his turn, almost half a century in exile, until he was invited back to become the first Karageorgević king. To me, however, he was the only person with heart and grace enough to offer a home to a tiny orphaned child, my grandfather, barely a few years old. Therefore, on this issue and many other larger issues, Peter was a great man.

I have heard some people say Peter may have murdered his wife when she was pregnant with their last child Andrew, that possibly he shoved her and she fell down a set of stairs, but this rumour is unsubstantiated. I have also heard others say Peter lived his years of exile as a drunk. But as I am learning with my research, all these Karageorgević men are surrounded by lewd and salacious gossip, some of it true, but most likely not all of it. How to assess a person's life, after all? By flimsy threads of unsubstantiated gossip? Or by the evident and very real and courageous acts with which they helped their fellow men? You decide what you will; my decision comes easily to me. I think the record speaks for itself. None of these men who put their own lives on the line can be questioned for their true determination. In my opinion the results of their lives outweigh any petty gossip.

When my grandfather Paul, unwanted by his parents, was sent to live with his uncle Peter in Switzerland – the head of the Karageorgević dynasty – Peter was languishing in Geneva. I do not doubt his circumstances were comfortable, but surely they were devoid of the comforts of a happy, loving home. Peter adored his wife, and her death, despite the circumstances, left him lonely and unhappy. Perhaps he drank too much. So what? Who wouldn't under the circumstances? Do you expect him to be juicing and jogging? And yet all his life was devoted to readying himself to take the helm of a country. He married appropriately, he had sons and heirs which was his duty, he waited patiently, and then, despite no promise of such an eventuality, one day his time came. The point was that when that day came he was ready for it and he returned to Serbia in a cloud of glory, riding through the streets in a golden carriage pulled by horses. When wars broke out he was at the front line on his white horse, whipping up the fervour of his troops and leading from the front. This was a brave man.

Peter was also bound by duty and he was clearly a good man. It was he, after all, who offered a home to my grandfather – his nephew Paul – when his brother Arsen could only think of engaging in war. Peter never remarried, which I believe shows his love for his deceased wife. He reared his children, Alexander, George and Helen, making sure they too went to the best schools to prepare them for a life at the helm of a country. Peter took his life and his obligations with great seriousness and for this he should be commended. He did not design his life around his own pleasures, but rather he worked stridently for the betterment of his legacy, for his ancestor Karageorge and for his descendants.

When in 1903 his uncle Peter took back the homeland, my grandfather, barely ten years old, was swept up and moved with him. Peter died in 1921 so obviously I never met him, but when I research his life I find endless photographs of King Peter, and there is my grandfather. When I see Paul he starts out as a very young boy with a look of horror on his otherwise solemn face, and then as an adolescent and later as a young man. All stages that are perfectly natural, and yet I realized I had never known him as anything other than a grandfather. These photos resonate with me. He is always standing adroitly to attention but in the background, or to the side, never promoted to front and centre, and I feel I can construe my grandfather's thoughts from that severe look on his face. I knew my grandfather personally and I can remember his resonant voice and his gentle mannerisms. When I picture him in my mind, I can see everything from his tweed suits to his shiny shoes to the quiet smile on his placid face. When I research his uncle, King Peter, a previously unknown world opens up for me of stills and footage, and repeatedly I see my grandfather at the edge of these shots, standing behind his uncle in the shadows, looking thoughtful, never smiling. It is this seriousness that is most at odds with my memories of him, which are all about gaiety, despite his formal nature.

King Peter's time in Serbia is well-documented, yet I find myself repeatedly stumbling into scenes that are new to me. No matter his age or dress, I always instantly recognize Paul by his soulful eyes and earnest, intense demeanour. Where others, in this case King Peter, have a look of conviction and confidence – almost of defiance – my grandfather never shares that look. He appears pensive, contemplative, as if he's thinking, and wondering just when and how he can get away. King Peter spent his life wanting nothing more than to be in Serbia but I believe my grandfather Paul wanted the exact opposite.

Reading history and bumping into family members is a fascinating experience. As I wade through the stories of distant relatives I've never met, some I have barely heard of, I start to discern familiar faces and anecdotes. I research photos of King Peter I or King Alexander I and my grandfather Prince Paul cautiously makes an appearance. Cautiously yet distinctively emerging, though always on the periphery; included and at the same time clearly apart. While his cousins wore grown-up military uniforms he was dressed in a child's cotton sailor suit and carrying a straw hat – a boater. Was this strictly due to his age? Or was this a subtle psychological diminution of his position in their lives, an indication of his insignificance, a way of keeping him in his place? They need not have concerned themselves; Paul wanted only to do his duty and beyond that he wanted a quiet civilian life.

While Peter was born in Belgrade, generally a good omen for a Karageorgević Serbian prince, soon his father and his family were despatched into exile. The curse of the Karageorgević clan! Yet Peter always knew his mission: put simply, to return and resume his place as the head of the House of Karageorgević. When word was sent to him, to his home in Switzerland, of the plot to assassinate the reigning monarchs, King Alexander I Obrenović and his consort Queen Draga, Peter wanted no part in this regicide. But he did not talk the plotters out of it. After the King and Queen were murdered, Peter moved with his family to Belgrade to take the reins of the country. He arrived ready to rule. A quick check on the Internet and you will find footage of his return in a fairy-tale carriage pulled by horses and surrounded by mounted guards with sabres and plumed hats.

One of the first documentaries ever made – or so I'm assured – was filmed by a couple of Brits from Sheffield; it records the elaborate procession in 1904 of King Peter, his family, retinue and army to the cathedral for his coronation. The cameras follow him after his exit from the church, mounted once more upon his fine white stallion and crowned with a massive headpiece of jewels and a cape of ermine as he parades through the streets of Belgrade, nodding to well-wishers in their finest clothes of long coats and top hats. Peter is followed by his sons Alexander and George, and while I cannot spot his brother Prince Arsen, I cannot believe he would miss such an event as this. In one frame, too blurry to be certain, I think I see my grandfather seated in an open carriage and adjusting his white cap. Since he is the only small child in the entire procession I imagine it must be him, but I cannot be sure. Squadrons of cavalry follow one after the other in their finest uniforms, some with swords held erect, others playing band instruments, and in between are open carriages with ladies in huge feathered hats. Then come six horses straining to pull a glorious cannon, to my eye already hopelessly outdated regarding warfare, but to the Serbian army clearly an object of enormous significance.

Long before this momentous day, in 1844, when Prince Alexander I of Serbia and his consort Princess Persida Nenadović were living in their Austro-Hungarian-designed palace in what was then the outskirts of Belgrade (and today is in a bustling residential neighbourhood) their baby Peter was born on a hot June day. Peter was born not only in the capital city of his homeland, but at a time when his own father was on the throne, signalling great things for him just as it had for his own father, Alexander, who started life under similar stars. Peter had a particular perspective about his rightful place as the natural future leader of Serbia. This would last until he was fourteen years old when his father was forced into exile. Life as he knew it was over, but as it would transpire and as he had always believed, not forever. In the meantime, the family repaired to the hilltop town of Temesvár on the Romanian border.

As a young man, Peter's mission was clear and, like his forebears, he was serious and disciplined. Going by the name Pierre Kara he attended school in France. In 1862 he enrolled at the well-known military academy, the École Spéciale Militaire de Saint-Cyr in Paris.

Keen to move beyond mere theory in 1871, Prince Peter volunteered in the Franco-Prussian war. Pierre Kara was commissioned into the French Foreign Legion, forming part of the army of the Loire. On 11 October he was wounded in battle near Orléans and taken prisoner by the Prussians. Prince Peter was dauntlessly brave and intrepid and, not allowing himself to be captured, he escaped by swimming across the Loire River in the dark of night. His grandfather would no doubt have been exceedingly proud. His exploits must surely have reached the ears of his younger brother Arsen who would have been fired up and filled with desire to throw himself into the fray. I am sure he could barely wait.

During the Great Eastern Crisis of 1875–78 in Bosnia and Herzegovina, a Serb set off an uprising against the continued stranglehold of the enduring Ottoman Empire. Then, in 1875, Prince Peter adopted the *nom de guerre* of Petar Mrkonjić and fought as a *hajduk* rebel, joining the Bosnian Serb insurgents as a leader of a guerrilla unit. News of his bravery spread across the country and, instead of being rewarded, he was expelled despite his excellence, or perhaps because of it, at the insistence of Prince Milan Obrenović, ruler of Serbia at that time. It can be presumed Obrenović saw Peter Karageorgević as a threat to his throne and feared Peter's popularity among the Serbian people.

Therefore, as article 10 of the 1869 Serbian Constitution stated, 'None of Karageorge's family nor any of his descendants can be elected as Serbian princes because they are a curse on the nation.'

Prince Milan's reaction to him was, in effect, an enormous compliment to Peter's charisma and natural leadership. Nevertheless, he was forced to leave the country. Again, I can hear the gnashing of teeth of Arsen, no doubt drowning with envy and desire to get his hands dirty with war. Peter and Arsen were Karageorgević to their marrow.

The Great Eastern crisis ended with the Congress of Berlin in 1878, through which Serbia finally gained full independence. In 1882, after some European negotiations, Serbia officially became a kingdom and Prince Milan Obrenović was crowned king. While Peter was forced to leave Serbia, he left as a war hero and one day he would return as such. To this day in the eyes of most Serbs his legacy is untainted and secure. Despite his prowess as a warrior, Prince Peter was also a romantic and in 1883 he married the love of his life, the beautiful young Princess Zorka of Montenegro. They married in her father's castle and the young couple lived in the mountains of Montenegro for a decade. Life in the mountains must have been somewhat blissful as Montenegro is famously beautiful. Still, Peter never took his eyes off Serbia and his true intentions.

Prince Peter and Princess Zorka had five children: Helen (1884–1962), Milena (1886–87), George (1887–1972) and Alexander (1888–1934); and in 1890 Zorka was pregnant again. She was twenty-five years old and here an abundance of rumours abound. Some say she died during the birth of her last child. Some say she met with an accident, a fall perhaps. Others say she was shoved, possibly even by Peter. For sure she died, how or from what exactly we do not know. Her baby, a boy they named Andrew, also died. Here again the rumours diverge, some saying little Andrew died during childbirth, other stories saying he died weeks later. Whatever the timing of these sad events, they left Peter wounded far deeper than any battle scars. Peter loved his wife and her death was life-altering for him. He immediately abandoned their home in Montenegro, never to return, and took his children with him. His actions suggest he probably was not responsible for killing her, as he obviously adored her and devoted himself to her while she was alive, but people love dirty gossip so the rancid versions persist. Let people believe what they will. It is not my job to say I know the definitive version, but when I look at how he lived his life I do not see a man who would have killed the wife he loved, the wife he never replaced.

He arranged for Zorka and her baby to be buried in the Church of St George in Topola, Serbia. After Zorka died, Peter had no further desire to remain in Montenegro and he moved away, first to Paris and then to Geneva where he settled. Peter's two sons were first sent to boarding schools in Switzerland and then George and Alexander were admitted to the Page Corps in St Petersburg. Meanwhile his only daughter, Helen, was sent to the Smolny Institute. The Smolny Institute was built in 1806–8 in accordance with a decree of Catherine II (Catherine the Great) in 1764. The Smolny was Russia's first educational establishment for women and continued to function under the personal patronage of the Russian empress until just before the 1917 revolution. It was at the personal invitation of Empress Alexandra that the young Princess Helen of Serbia attended the Smolny Institute. The building would later be repurposed as Lenin's headquarters.

Princess Elena, another of Zorka's younger sisters, married the Prince of Naples, who would later become King Victor Emmanuel III of Italy, making her the Queen of Italy, among many other illustrious titles including, briefly, Empress of Ethiopia. Queen Elena was loved by the people of Italy for her selfless work on behalf of the sick and the poor. In 1919, to save the life of an endangered Romanov, she arranged for a boat to be sent to the Crimea to fetch the Grand Duchess Maria Pavlovna (the grandmother of my grandmother Olga). The boat docked and the Grand Duchess, upon seeing it, declared it was too disgustingly filthy and no place for a Grand Duchess so she refused to board. The boat was put back to sea where it promptly sank, drowning everyone aboard. A second boat was sent which the Grand Duchess agreed was befitting her imperial standards and on this vessel she sailed away to safety.

Elena and Victor Emmanuel were the last royal rulers of Italy (except for a single month in 1946 when their son Umberto reigned), seeing it through two world wars and losing their rights to a referendum. The future must have seemed clear as daylight when they could not save their own daughter Mafalda, who was captured by the Germans and sent to Buchenwald concentration camp. Despite their efforts to free her, ironically, Mafalda was killed by the Allies. She died in 1944 from injuries suffered during an Allied bombing of a munitions factory inside the Buchenwald concentration camp.

The Italian royal family, the House of Savoy, was permanently expelled from Italy in 1946. The King spent the last few months of his life in Egypt, where he expired in 1947. The King's eldest child, HRH Princess Maria Pia of Savoy, would one day marry Prince Alexander of Yugoslavia, eldest son of Prince Paul, and they made their home in Paris in the 1950s and 1960s. Paris was to be the meeting ground of uprooted royals from all over Europe, like that wonderful scene in *Candide* where the former kings and queens sit about in a cafe and debate what could have been. Ah, philosophy versus reality. So many branches of my family lived out the theories of philosophers in their own Theatre of the Absurd, except it was their real lives. Such are the ups and downs of royalty and dynasties. Beware, I say to the dreamers.

However, long before all that, and before the end of the nineteenth century, Peter's youngest brother Arsen had not only pulled off a spectacular marriage to the hugely wealthy Princess and Countess Aurora Demidoff di San Donato, he had produced an heir – his son Paul. Back in Belgrade, conspirators – tired of the inept rule of King Alexander I Obrenović and his despised barren older wife Draga – were plotting. With the excuse of the childless marriage creating a vacancy for succession, the plotters settled on their first choice, the candidacy of Peter Karageorgević, then living as an ordinary citizen in Geneva. Mentally, of course, Peter was nowhere near ordinary, because no ordinary citizen pines for a crown he is convinced belongs to him.

One day, and not at his urging, Peter was informed by a delegation sent to visit him at his home in Switzerland that he was their choice of candidate to rule the country. They asked him to return as their ruler. Of course the notion of ruling Serbia would have appealed to Peter, but he wanted no part in overthrowing the current regime. He never had any plans or intentions of toppling the ruling Obrenović King. Peter made it abundantly clear to these plotters he would not collude with regicide. Nevertheless, the conspirators returned to Belgrade and they initiated their plans to assassinate King Alexander and Queen Draga.

Many differing reports exist as to the exact events of that very ugly night. What is well known is that the King and Queen were discovered by the conspirators hiding, praying and trembling in a closet in their bedroom. After Alexander and Draga, who were only partially dressed, revealed themselves, the assassins attacked. The Queen tried to save her husband's life by blocking his body with her own right before both were shot multiple times and then savagely hacked to pieces. Their mutilated bodies were tossed from a second floor window to bespatter the palace courtyard. And here their remains were left to rot in the open air; a welcome reminder of regime change, the old-fashioned way. Later that same night, Queen Draga's brothers, considered too politically influential, were also killed along with key ministers, all of them gunned down in their homes.

Immediately, members of the new interim government gathered and the National Assembly met in session on 4 June 1903 where they voted Peter Karageorgević King of Serbia and an entourage was sent to Geneva to escort him back. He ascended the Serbian throne as Peter I, elected as the King of Serbia by the Serbian parliament and senate. After forty-five years in exile, the Karageorgević dynasty had regained the throne from the rival House of Obrenović.

The news of the overthrow was received with mixed feelings by the Serbs. More of a problem, however, was the swift international outrage over the bloody coup. Russia and Austria-Hungary vehemently condemned the barbaric assassinations. The United Kingdom, the United States and the Netherlands withdrew their ambassador equivalents from Serbia – freezing diplomatic relations – and imposed sanctions which were not lifted until 1905.

Inside the country, the Western-educated king got right to work and attempted to liberalize Serbia with the goal of creating a Western-style constitutional monarchy. As a young man he had translated John Stuart Mill's *On Liberty* into Serbian. Peter had a lot of sound ideas and a total commitment to his cause. King Peter I gradually became extremely popular for his dedication to parliamentary democracy. He paid two solemn state visits to St Petersburg and Paris in 1910 and 1911 respectively, and was greeted as a hero of both democracy and national independence in the troublesome Balkans.

The reign of King Peter I Karageorgević from 1903–14 is remembered as a 'golden age' due to unrestricted political freedom, free press, and cultural ascendancy among southern Slavs. King Peter I was supportive of the movement of pan-Slav unification and hosted various cultural gatherings in Belgrade.

King Peter I gained enormous popularity following the Balkan Wars in 1912 and 1913 which, from a Serb and southern Slav perspective, were great successes, heralded by the spectacular military victories over the Ottomans, followed by the liberation of Old Serbia (Vilayet of Kosovo) and mostly Slavic-inhabited Macedonia (Vilayet of Monastir). The territory of Serbia was doubled and her prestige among southern Slavs (Croats and Slovenes in particular, as well as among the Serbs in Austria-Hungary, Bosnia and Herzegovina, Vojvodina, the Military Frontier, Dalmatia and Slavonia) grew significantly, with Peter I as the main symbol of both this political and historical success.

After a conflict between military and civilian representatives in the spring of 1914, King Peter chose to retire due to ill health, reassigning his royal prerogative to his second son, Crown Prince Alexander. This son, Alexander, had been groomed for many years as the true successor and future for Serbia. Alongside his father, he had governed in his elevated status as heir apparent.

Did Peter lead the way for Alexander to see that he had an opportunity to claim the realm? Was it Peter who chose Alexander over his older son George? Was this marginalizing of George a mere matter of politics? After all, Peter's brother Arsen was clearly a great warrior but was he too great? Was this why he too was shoved to the side? A day would come when Arsen was formally banished from Serbia while his nephew was on the throne. Was everything about maintaining power and keeping those who might steal it sidelined and in the shadows?

Older brother George, for a variety of reasons, deferred his position to his younger brother Alexander. Some say this was because of bad choices he made as a youth, which included an incident that resulted in the death of his servant, but it was also due to his quick temper and unsteady nature. Whatever the cause, George, who for a portion of his life would be locked up in a mental institution, would be the only member of the Karageorgević family never to leave the country after World War II; once freed from the confinement of the mental hospital he remained in Topola until his death in 1973. George was enormously popular with the people who knew him. He lived the life of a regular citizen and was much loved and talk of his mental instability is challenged by many who knew him personally.

All this was despite the country's political departure into communism. Even more interesting is that apparently Marshal Tito not only personally liked George, he also arranged an allowance for him, and a car and driver befitting his strange, suspended position. While the rest of the family were advised they would be killed if they set foot on Yugoslav land as 'enemies of the State',

George lived out his life in his homeland. It was a very unusual circumstance for a Karageorgević, but certainly a lifestyle I hope will resume, at least for my own generation and those to follow.

But this is a new Serbia and in the days of Marshal Tito it was understood our family was not welcome. Such was the legend I was raised with, and my cousins too, it dampened our enthusiasm for visiting the fatherland. George was liked and respected by Serbs who saw him live a normal life. People I have met and spoken with in Topola whose grandparents personally knew George say the stories of his mental imbalance are fiction, or at least greatly exaggerated, and I was advised to more closely examine the sources of these rumours, rather than to believe them, and certainly not to perpetuate them.

King Peter exerted minimal interference in politics, looking toward peace rather than war for solutions. Equally, he did not wish to aggravate the Black Hand, a notorious rebel organization which had become increasingly powerful. Rumours abound that the Black Hand was directly funded by certain Italians working through foreign (i.e. Bosnian) operatives. The Italians had their own objectives for wanting to destabilize the Austro-Hungarian Empire and redraw the borders of the Balkans. In response to the Austro-Hungarian annexation of Bosnia and Herzegovina, in 1914 the Black Hand would order the assassination of Archduke Franz Ferdinand at Sarajevo, inadvertently starting World War I.

The King, at this stage of his life, with his health weakened, spent most of his time in various Serbian spas. Though he remained relatively inactive during World War I, he never took his attention fully off world events and occasionally, when the military situation became critical, he visited trenches on the front line to inspire the morale of his troops. A memorable visit in 1915 involved King Peter, by then seventy-one, picking up a rifle and shooting at enemy soldiers.

The moment is recalled by the British diplomat Sir Nevile Henderson in his book *Water Under the Bridges*:

> King Peter had been ill and handed over the government to Prince Alexander as regent. Despite his frail health King Peter was intent on rousing his troops. Mounted on a white horse he reviewed his troops and told them that though he would understand if any of them desired to go back to their homes, he himself was determined to die rather than to yield. The effect on the Serbian army was immediate and electrifying. On the night of 2nd December it began its great counter offensive. For 11 days it advanced without a halt, driving the Austrians before it. On the 13th it re-entered Belgrade and by that evening there were no Austrians left on Serbian soil, except for over 60,000 prisoners.

Following the invasion of Serbia by the joint forces of Germany, Austria-Hungary and Bulgaria in October 1915, King Peter I led the army and tens of thousands of civilian refugees through the high mountains of Albania to the Adriatic Sea. This was a monumental effort that took many soldiers' lives, and nearly his own too.

After the dramatic march through harsh winter conditions, via the hostile environment of the Albanian highlands, and at a cost of more than 100,000 lives, the King and his army, exhausted by cold and famine, were eventually transported by the Allies in mostly French ships to Corfu in early 1916. King Peter I, already in very poor health, remained on the Greek isle of Corfu, which became the seat of the Serbian government in exile until December 1918. The sea around the beautiful Greek island was nicknamed the Blue Graveyard.

In 1913 King Peter's nephew, Prince Paul, was in his first year at Oxford University, but as soon as the war began he formally excused himself and went dispiritedly yet directly to Serbia. Whatever his personal thoughts were about this, he was drilled in the concept of duty first and whether he liked it or not he set off. His university studies were officially postponed and he donned his military uniform and assumed his official position back in Belgrade. In 1916 he joined his uncle in Corfu and worked with the Red Cross. Paul was always a part of things, always drawn by what he believed was his duty, although his contributions seem never to have been much appreciated, if even noticed.

On 1 December 1918, King Peter I was proclaimed King of the Serbs, Croats and Slovenes. He remained abroad until July 1919 before finally returning to Belgrade where he died in 1921 at the age of seventy-seven. King Peter I is remembered for his modesty, moderation and ardent patriotism. He was responsible for the construction of Oplenac, the family crypt at the Church of St George at Topola.

I placed a rose on his marble tomb.

9

HM King Alexander I of Yugoslavia

16 December 1888 – 9 October 1934

THE SECOND SON OF KING PETER AND PRINCESS ZORKA was Alexander Karageorgević. Alexander was born on 16 December 1888 in the Principality of Montenegro, the name-sake of his grandfather Prince Alexander I of Serbia. A mere thirty years earlier in 1858, Prince Alexander had been forced to abdicate and with his family flee to safety, thus surrendering power in Serbia to the rival House of Obrenović until the start of the next century.

Alexander's mother, Princess Zorka of Montenegro, the eldest daughter of Prince Nicholas of Montenegro, had sisters as beautiful as herself and all of them made rather spectacular marriages. These unions brought them face to face with great highs and mortal dangers. They lived extraordinary lives, but perhaps they expected as much.

Despite enjoying support from imperial Russia, when Alexander was born and during his early childhood, the Karageorgević family was in political exile; a disconnected diaspora with many relatives scattered all across Europe. They were condemned as enemies of the state and not welcome in Serbia; their own country had recently changed from a principality to a kingdom during this second Obrenović rule which enjoyed strong support from Austria-Hungary. The antagonism between the two rival royal houses was such that after the assassination of Prince Mihailo Obrenović in 1868 (an event in which certain Karageorgević family members were suspected of taking part), the Obrenović line resorted to making constitutional changes, specifically proclaiming the Karageorgević family banned from entering Serbia and stripping them of civic rights.

In 1890 Alexander was all of two years old when his mother, Princess Zorka, died from complications while giving birth to his younger brother Andrew. There are conflicting stories suggesting why or exactly when Zorka and her baby died. I will only say I hope it was natural causes. Alexander spent his first few years in Montenegro at the castle of his maternal grandparents. He experienced a trajectory similar to his own father and his grandfather, born one place and soon despatched to another, his life directed by the forces of political intrigue and life's pitfalls. At the exact same time, each was faced with circumstances that could easily have dismantled their confidence. Little Alexander's earliest years might have seemed idyllic, but with the death of his mother and his baby brother all he knew unravelled around him. Mercifully, he was too young, I presume, to know exactly what was going on, but it was a repetition of the fate of Karageorgević leaders, with one foot in the past and the other unsteadily searching for somewhere to wait out the perils of the day and always preparing for a certain future, regardless of shifting loyalties and landscapes. Is it a Serbian trait to believe so deeply against all provable odds?

Is that what kept them coming back, like waves to the shore? I cannot help but question this indestructible belief.

Alexander's father, Peter Karageorgević, having retreated into a depression following the death of his wife and infant son, gathered his children and moved first to Paris before settling in Geneva. Alexander and his brother George completed their elementary education in Switzerland.

At some point during the 1890s a pale, quiet boy not yet two years old came to live with Peter's family in Geneva. He was introduced as their cousin Paul, Prince of Serbia, and had travelled from St Petersburg, along with his nursemaid. He spoke mostly Russian and was shy, asking repeatedly where his mother was. These entreaties were overheard by Peter's sister-in-law Princess Elena of Montenegro who felt for the child and while it seems no one else paid him much attention, Aunt Elena took him under her wing. All his life, a strange life at that, Paul would be openly neglected by those closest to him and yet emotionally taken care of by peripheral angels.

In keeping with tradition, Peter sent his children – George, Alexander and their sister Helen – to polish their education at the Imperial Page Corps in St Petersburg for boys, and the Smolny Institute for girls, respectively. Little Paul, after a few years in Geneva, no doubt wished fervently he too could be sent to the only home he had known in St Petersburg where presumably he might be able to find his mother of whom he dreamt and for whom he pined. Instead, he would be torn from his Russian nursemaid, his only link to love, and placed in the hated Swiss boarding school.

In 1903, Alexander's father, Peter, representing the House of Karageorgević, took the Serbian throne after forty-five years of exile. Peter, aged fifty-eight, became King Peter I of Serbia, prompting George and Alexander's arrival in Serbia to finish their studies and also, not too subtly, place them in line for their turn at the helm. Their sister Helen, as a female, was around but given less attention, not out of any disrespect to her but rather as a product of the times and mores of the country. However, Paul was mostly unmentioned. He was certainly included, but repeatedly sidelined. There exists a photograph of the four children posing together, with my grandfather lying strangely at an angle in the foreground, as if someone intended to edit him from the picture. His melancholy mien suggests he is aware of this.

Meanwhile, young Helen remained in Russia, ignoring the stirrings of revolt, and in 1911 married Prince Ioann Konstantinovich of Russia, a member of the Romanov imperial family. Her brothers George and Alexander, however, returned to Belgrade and were very much front and centre.

As previously noted, while the dynasty did not cleave to the idea of primogeniture, and although they would never consider a female for a leader, they reserved the right to select from the worthiest of sons to carry on the dynasty. Thus, Alexander, the younger brother who was made of more substantial material than his older brother George, was considered the better choice for succession.

Alexander was thus prepared, schooled and trained in the ways of governance, kingdoms and politics. Ably proving himself in the First Balkan War in 1912 as commander of the First Army, Crown Prince Alexander fought victorious battles in Kumanovo and Bitola; and later, in 1913, during the Second Balkan War at the Battle of Bregalnica. After the Turks' withdrawal from Skopje, Prince Alexander was met, according to tradition, with flowers by the local people. From a young age, in other words, he had a taste of what it meant to lead. His certainty of his place in the world was reinforced by what he saw and how he was treated. There was no need or room for doubt.

In the aftermath of the Second Balkan War, Prince Alexander took sides in the complicated power struggle over how Macedonia should be administered. In this, Alexander bested Col. Dragutin 'Apis' Dimitrijević and in the wake of this, Alexander's father, King Peter, agreed to hand over royal powers to his son. On 24 June 1914 Alexander became Prince Regent of Serbia until the death of his father. In 1921 Alexander became king. It must all have seemed perfectly natural, preordained and expected. He knew the dangers but he would have scoffed at them, so sure was he of his place on Earth.

At the start of World War I Alexander was the nominal Supreme Commander of the Serbian army – true command was in the hands of the Chief of Staff of Supreme Headquarters, a position held by Stepa Stepanović (during the mobilization), Radomir Putnik (1914–15), Petar Bojović (1916–17) and Živojin Mišić (1918). The Serbian army distinguished itself in the battles at Cer and at the Drina (the Battle of Kolubara) in 1914, scoring victories against the invading Austro-Hungarian forces and evicting them from the country. The Karageorgević men – Peter, his younger brother Arsen and Peter's children Alexander and George, and even my grandfather Paul – all did their part. They rallied troops, encouraged their men and, I might add, unlike some armchair military men who for the sake of diplomacy shall go unnamed here, led from the front.

Foreign countries looked to benefit from the chaos and in broad daylight on 28 June 1914 a member of the Black Hand infamously assassinated Archduke Franz Ferdinand. The Black Hand was a secret school for assassins, purportedly funded by the Italians. The Italians were intent on redrawing borders and while looking to foment and distract world attention, it is doubtful their intention was to ignite a world war. More likely they hoped to send up a distracting flare, but instead set off the entire stockade of explosives. This act of terrorism inevitably pitched Austria-Hungary into war against Serbia. Russia moved in to protect their tiny ally and the rest, as they say, is history.

In 1915 the Serbian army was led by the ageing King Peter I and Crown Prince Alexander and they suffered many losses, being attacked from all directions by the alliance of Germany, Austria-Hungary and Bulgaria – a country always looking to gain more territory. The Serbian army withdrew through the gorges of Montenegro and northern Albania and eventually to the Greek island of Corfu, where it was reorganized and set up as a de facto Serbia. Once the army was regrouped and reinforced, it achieved a decisive victory on the Macedonian front at Kajmakčalan. The Serbian army carried out a major part in the final Allied breakthrough on the Macedonian front in the autumn of 1918.

For all involved, despite the propaganda, war was always about redrawing borders. A major factor was the Italians using their overreaching Black Hand to reconfigure the Balkans. Every schoolchild knows the British and the French were deep in each other's pockets, ready to sketch out new territories as far away as the Middle East. These details are so easily overlooked and instead all eyes are, erroneously, on the fabled Serbian 'aggression' regardless of the truth. History is a malleable story, the story of whomever is writing that particular round-up of self-serving 'facts'. It is my job here to tell it like it was, even though I do not expect a round of applause from all those double-dealing, scheming, self-important, self-righteous historians!

Meanwhile, Alexander's vision never wavered; on the contrary, his commitment to Serbia was strengthened and defined. For his part, on 1 December 1918, he received a delegation of the People's Council of Slovenes, Croats and Serbs. An address was read out by one of the delegation, and Alexander made a speech in acceptance. This was considered to be the birth of the Kingdom of Serbs, Croats and Slovenes. The subtle rearrangements of the names of the countries was no typographical accident; rather it was an indication of Alexander's vision and ambition.

In 1921, after the death of his father, Alexander inherited the throne of the Kingdom of Serbs, Croats and Slovenes, which from its inception was colloquially known both in the kingdom and the rest of Europe as Yugoslavia, loosely meaning 'unified southern Slavs'.

Karageorgević men marry well-heeled princesses and Alexander would be no different. On 8 June 1922 he married Princess Maria of Romania, a daughter of King Ferdinand of Romania, in Belgrade. Alexander and Maria had three sons: Crown Prince Peter, and princes Tomislav (here he is, the Tomislav of my youth and my connection to Zeljka!) and Andrej. On the home front, Alexander, intent on herding the unwieldy and nationalistic political Slavic cats of his parliament, exerted evermore control. Faced endlessly with nationalistic squabbling and dissent he became all the more autocratic, since there was no other way to govern the ungovernable. Meanwhile he kept his family out of politics.

And then, perhaps inevitably, the smouldering tinderbox of antagonism and differing sentiments blew up. Early in 1928, a pro-unification Serbian politician fatally shot three anti-unification Croatian politicians and wounded two others. Nationalism was threatening to tear asunder the fragile union that was Yugoslavia, which was always more of a concept than a workable reality and certainly not supported by its members.

As a response to the political crisis triggered by the assassination in parliament of Croatian politician Stjepan Radić, King Alexander abolished the constitution on 6 January 1929, prorogued the parliament and introduced a personal dictatorship (the so-called January 6th Dictatorship; *Šestojanuarska diktatura*). He also changed the name of the country to the Kingdom of Yugoslavia and changed the internal divisions from the thirty-three *oblasts* (counties) to nine new *banovinas* (districts) on 3 October. With regards to his political restructuring, it was obvious he saw no other way to manage the volatile vying factions with their deep-rooted nationalistic perspectives. This would prove futile as the divisions were too long-standing and too deep-rooted. This would become apparent a long time later in the 1990s when, without the governance of a strong hand, neighbours tore into neighbours resulting in a bloody mess.

In 1931, giving up any pretence of sharing power with those intent only in furthering personal goals instead of the greater good, Alexander decreed a new constitution. This transferred executive power to the King. This was not what he set out to do but what he decided had to be done because obviously there was no other effective way. Elections were to be by universal male suffrage. The provision for a secret ballot was dropped and pressure on public employees to vote for the governing party was to be a feature of all elections held under Alexander's constitution. Furthermore, the King would appoint half the upper house directly, and legislation could become law with the approval of one of the houses alone if it were also approved by the King. Thus, despite the best of intentions, a new style of leadership was born. Allegedly, in November 1932, Alexander said, 'If you want to [...] cause a regime change, you need to kill me.'

~

The investigation into any segment of history is always interesting though usually somewhat remote, more like fairy tales than reality. King Alexander was one such enigma to me. Forging a loop with this fraught history came to pass on my second trip to Serbia, in the autumn of 2014. On this second and far longer trip to the homeland, I visited a monument which the King had commissioned on a mountain overlooking Belgrade, with views of many miles of cultivated valleys in all directions. The Tomb of the Unknown Soldier at Avala, begun in 1922, was a project Alexander would never see completed. The monument was intended to commemorate the brave participants of both the Balkan Wars and World War I – wars he fought valiantly in alongside his brother and his father.

King Alexander's way of life and manner of thought is as remote to me as this tomb which was built on the site of an old fort, which was itself built over the ruins of an ancient Roman city; the daisy-chain layers of history casually holding us all together. Over time, perhaps in conjunction with his declaring himself leader, Alexander's ambitions for this tomb expanded to become an enormous complex requiring the freeing up of space on the mountaintop.

~

As with most Serbs, Alexander was highly superstitious and after three deaths of family members occurring on a Tuesday, he refused to undertake public functions on that day of the week. However, circumstances were sometimes beyond his control. Thus it was on Tuesday, 9 October 1934 that King Alexander of Yugoslavia was in Marseilles to begin an official state visit to France, essentially to strengthen the alliance known as the Little Entente. While Alexander slowly motored in an open car through the thronged streets, seated beside the French Foreign Minister, Louis Barthou, a gunman – the Bulgarian Vlado Chernozemski – stepped forward and shot the King twice with a Mauser C96 semi-iautomatic pistol. Alexander died in the car, slumped backwards in the seat, with his eyes open and blood running down his chin.

This assassination was one of the first to be captured on film; the shooting occurred directly in front of the cameraman. While the exact moment of the bullet entering the King's head was not recorded, the events leading up to the killing and the immediate aftermath can be seen frame by frame. The body of the chauffeur (who had been killed instantly) became jammed against the brakes of the car, allowing the cameraman to continue filming within inches of the King for a number of minutes afterwards. I watched this footage over and over, finding it deeply disturbing. It was heartbreaking, to tell you the truth, because first one sees the King seated, confidently smiling and waving at the crowds and then, in an instant, his life is extinguished; his head has collapsed and his body is lifeless, spilling blood.

The assassin was a member of the Bulgarian Internal Macedonian Revolutionary Organization (IMRO or VMRO) and an experienced sharpshooter. Immediately after shooting King Alexander, Chernozemski was slashed to death by the sword of a mounted French policeman, and then ripped to shreds by the crowd. By the time King Alexander was removed from the scene, he and the French minister Barthou were already long since dead.

The IMRO was a political organization which fought for the secession of Vardar Macedonia from Yugoslavia and was looking, once again, to become part of the Kingdom of Bulgaria. The leader of the organization at that time was Ivan Mihailov and the IMRO worked in alliance with the Croatian Ustaše group led by Ante Pavelić, the Ustaše being an arm of Hitler's Nazis, and equally lethal. Chernozemski and three Croatian accomplices had travelled to France from Hungary via Switzerland. Although there is no concrete evidence that either the Italian dictator Benito Mussolini or the Hungarian government were directly involved in the plot, the public opinion in Yugoslavia was that Italy, via Croatia and its Ustaše, had been instrumental in the planning and directing of the assassination. The incident was later used by Yugoslavia as an argument to counter the Croatian attempts of secession, and Italian and Hungarian revisionism.

The footage recording Alexander's assassination remains one of the most notable pieces of newsreel in existence, alongside the film of Tsar Nicholas II of Russia's coronation, the funerals of Queen Victoria of the United Kingdom and Emperor Franz Joseph I of Austria, and the assassination of US President John F. Kennedy.

The very next day the body of King Alexander I was transported to the port of Split, Croatia by the Yugoslav destroyer JRM *Dubrovnik*. After a huge funeral in Belgrade attended by approximately 500,000 people and many leading European statesmen,

Alexander was interred in the mausoleum at Oplenac. The Holy See gave special permission to bishops to attend the funeral in an Orthodox church.

Unknown to the public, King Alexander I had an enormous heraldic eagle tattooed across his chest. Also unknown to anyone were King Alexander's plans for the future because he never let anyone in on this classified information, even his family. He kept his intentions to himself.

The secret Alexander took to his death, though not to his tomb, was penned in a letter which was enclosed in a stamped wax-sealed envelope, intended to be read by his cousin Prince Paul. The only official political information imparted to Prince Paul by his cousin during his lifetime was that in the event of the King's untimely death, he was to search the King's royal desk at the palace and find this envelope. With melodramatic overtones on a level with any creepy Hollywood film, my grandfather would discover the plan in that letter.

10

HM King Peter II of Yugoslavia

6 September 1923 – 3 November 1970

AND

HRH Crown Prince Alexander of Yugoslavia

b. 17 July 1945

KING PETER II, THOUGH ONLY SEVENTEEN YEARS OLD, WAS the last Karageorgević monarch to remain in Serbia after the coup of 27 March 1941. This was not his decision to make, but it is what happened. Peter's uncle the regent Prince Paul and his wife Princess Olga along with their small daughter Jelisaveta (Elizabeth) were ordered to leave, under threat of execution. Paul and Olga's two older sons, Alexander and Nicholas, were at boarding school in England, and therefore out of harm's way. Alexander, nicknamed Schultz, was close friends with the young Peter, perhaps his only friend his own age, even if their temperaments were drastically different: Peter was quiet and thoughtful whereas Schultz was boisterous. I find it a small comfort to know they had each other to some degree, although Peter was home-schooled by his tutor Cecil Parrott and Alexander was sent off to boarding school.

Given twenty-four hours to get out of the country permanently, Paul, Olga and little Jelisaveta hastily travelled to Athens, to Olga's childhood home of Tatoi Palace where for an instant they felt safe. They might have stayed there except Churchill and Anthony Eden found the flimsiest of excuses to push them out and set them adrift on a course that would wreck the next decade of their lives.

Meanwhile, Peter, all of seventeen years old, was established as the King and thrust to the forefront of international politics. Soon Hitler would invade and behind the scenes Churchill and Eden manipulated all their puppets as they played off the Serbian military, led by staunch royalist General Draža Mihailović, and rival communist Marshal Tito. While the Germans bombed the Slavs, causing utter destruction and countless deaths, still the Brits toyed with who they might prefer to back.

At the same time, the Special Operations Executive (SOE) had been ably penetrated by the Soviets and Tito was pushed forward as the better choice. Randolph Churchill, Winston's son, tasked with sorting out the fate of the Balkans, fell in love with Tito, though some would say he was led by the nose by the calculating Russians. Eventually General Draža Mihailović was captured by the communists and imprisoned and ultimately sentenced to death in 1946. The issue of rehabilitating the name of Serbia's war hero General Mihailović was in the courts for many years. Finally, while I was writing this book, the Supreme Court of Cassation rehabilitated General Mihailović.

Thus, Marshal Tito was installed as the head of the country to lead it whichever way he pleased. And he pleased himself with disavowing the rigid style of Russian communism. He moved himself and his family into the now empty palaces and hunting lodges of the deposed Karageorgević family, going so far as to invite the heads of state of foreign countries to come stay with him in his new magnificence. And they did.

By the summer of 1941 seventeen-year-old Peter was in name a king, though not yet of age to order a drink in a bar, or make any decisions of his own. His mind was filled with elaborate schemes of complex travels. He was told he would first go to Athens, and next Jerusalem, then on to Cairo where a huge British delegation was forever pulling strings and running the show. Eventually he was assured he would safely get to London, and from there they would reload the cannons of their true path to get him home to Yugoslavia and back in the saddle as king. Was any of this ever truly going to happen? Of course not, because it was all a lie, and easily sold to the gullible child-king who was by now totally isolated from his family and surrounded by a dangerous cabal of seasoned cynical politicians with their own decidedly fixed interests, none of whom put him anywhere near the centre of their plans.

All this was with the purported intention of setting him up, this manipulated child; with promises to get him home to Yugoslavia. But this 'country' of Yugoslavia, this conglomerate of opposing views and nationalities and even languages, was already long gone, gripped by the hands of a new regime with a new governmental structure and ideology. It was all a lie and King Peter, not yet of age, believed every mendacious word. And why wouldn't he? He was raised to trust his British 'friends', and it would be a long time before he knew what had happened to him. Despite Peter's entrenched trust in his British 'friends', all these impressive promises collapsed – dust in the wind of reality, replaced with the very real actions of the salivating hounds of war, marching soldiers right into their graves, as the powers sought for gains of their own. It was exactly what my grandfather had stalled and delayed as long as possible, because he knew many Slavs would unnecessarily lose their lives. He had done what he could to avoid it and, despite everything, it was happening. Senseless death. At this time, Prince Paul and his wife and child wandered from Egypt to Kenya searching for a place to call home until things improved. Against them were Churchill and Eden, cruelly intent on finding my grandfather a home in exile – like Napoleon on Elba – where he could disappear or die; they did not care which.

Meanwhile in London, along with a contingent of other distressed exiles, Peter met his soon-to-be bride, Princess Alexandra of Greece. They were the same age, in their early twenties, and they were in similar circumstances – destitute refugees reliant on government handouts and the generosity of wealthy new friends. It must have felt like an enormous relief to have found each other; two castaways on an island in the foaming centre of the fallout of World War II which raged around them, the outcome still far-off and unknowable. Mercifully they had each other, and inevitably they threw in their lot together and were married in 1944.

When King Peter II and his consort, Alexandra, were expecting their first, and as it would happen their only, child, Crown Prince Alexander, arrangements were made for the birth to occur in room number 212 at the hotel Claridge's. The British authorities along with Yugoslav representatives set up this room, theoretically like an embassy, granting it Yugoslav sovereignty.

Thus, like wizards in a Broadway production, someone thought to dust the floor of room 212 with a handful of Serbian soil, tossing it about and thereby establishing 'Little Yugoslavia'. The Brits with their phantasmagorical foreign policy arranged for this magic trick to be performed. They were, after all, always entirely in charge.

In 1945 Crown Prince Alexander was born in room 212. The purpose of temporarily reassigning the room as sovereign Yugoslavia was so that one day ostensibly the Crown Prince could maintain his Yugoslav nationality. This was to maintain the charade with young King Peter that the Brits meant what they said to him about getting him home, which of course was not true. Thus, Peter was repeatedly deceived as to the real intentions of his British hosts, who never at any time cared a jot for him to return to Yugoslavia, a country Churchill deemed a 'sideshow', and a place only useful as a bargaining tool, a chip with which to negotiate over spoils. But Peter was only twenty or twenty-one, entirely beguiled by his hosts and he would have believed whatever they told him. This was despite his Uncle Paul's ignominious removal as regent, the country having suffered a full scale and very bloody civil war, then being carpet-bombed by the Germans, and subsequently handed over to militant communists. Yugoslavia, as a kingdom, was for all intents and purposes, a lost cause.

These days Crown Prince Alexander recounts, with a touch of nostalgia, that as a grown-up he went back to see room 212 where he was born, and he says it is impressively grand, more a comfortable apartment than a hotel room. It is airy and spacious with a capacious bedroom, a vast sitting room, separate dining room, separate kitchen and a massive luxurious bathroom. Now,

all these years later, it is officially named the Prince Alexander
Suite.

King Peter, his bride, Alexandra, and their baby boy lived on in
England, at the behest of their hosts. Where else should they go?
In very real terms they were far from their respective homelands
to which they were forbidden to return. They were truly homeless, frighteningly penniless and, thanks to the miasma of lies
they were fed, they were entirely directionless, unless you count
the grotesque fallacy that they were heading home to Yugoslavia.

Behind their backs – and this would be exposed years later in
documents brought to public attention by my mother Princess
Elizabeth of Yugoslavia – this young couple and their baby boy
were deemed too dangerous to house and were encouraged to
move on, shoved along to the new world of America. Naturally
they did as they were told – they really had no choice – and thus
they wound up in New York City. It would be a long time before
Crown Prince Alexander would discover what all this chaos was
about. For him it was just his life.

In 1948, when he was three, Alexander's parents moved with
him and his nanny to New York City and they installed themselves
in rooms at the Carlyle Hotel on the Upper East Side, Madison
Avenue and 76th Street. The rooms they took were for themselves.
Their young son, Crown Prince Alexander, was placed in a rented
apartment directly across the street with his nanny.

On some evenings, young Alexander was escorted across
Madison Avenue by his nanny to say goodnight to his parents.
This frequently involved long waits in a hallway outside the
closed front door of their hotel suite. Sometimes the little boy
took to pouring glasses of water down the mail chute, displaying
small acts of defiance at his peculiar treatment. The hotel staff

were not thrilled with him, but in his own way he was asserting himself, acting out his displeasure because on a fundamental level he knew this was not right. Still, he always loved and respected his parents and when they were together they were charming with him. It was just the gross infrequency with which he saw them that was inescapably evident, and he felt it.

Apparently King Peter II would tell his wife stories about how they had to get ready to meet with important types, as they were due to dine with General Electric and General Motors but these were merely jokes, perhaps to alleviate his own sense of displacement, perhaps to bolster his unrealistic belief that all he did was plot and plan his road home. Maybe it helped to give him hope. But the young and tender Princess Alexandra would believe him and not understand he was kidding. In retrospect it seems that while perhaps Peter's sense of humour kept him going, maybe even preserved his sanity during a time of total craziness, it was one more factor wearing away at the already frayed nerves of his fragile bride – a product of Greek upheavals and repeated exiles. This fragility would eventually show itself. Though not quite yet.

Crown Prince Alexander remembers many crossings of the Atlantic by boat; once on the *Queen Mary*, another time on the *Queen Elizabeth*; and also possibly once on a ship named the *United States*. He vividly recalls these long ocean crossings, no doubt to meet up with his parents, his father always on the hunt for one more meeting that would restore things to how they once were. He was a child really, just trying to put his life back to a time when he was happy, a small child with both his parents in his homeland. That was all he wanted, and his tunnel vision was his fuel. Life in New York was never meant to be forever, and eventually the urgency to speed up getting 'home' to Yugoslavia may have encouraged the family's return to Europe.

One can imagine the young king engaging Americans in conversations regarding his need to get home to Yugoslavia and them staring blankly at him, 'What? Where?' These Americans must have thought him nuts to want to leave their brave new world of opportunity and modernity, to return to what? Some medieval, savage, war-torn backwater? As much as it must have seemed incomprehensible to them, America and all its promise must have seemed a lustreless dead end for the young king, fervently on his mission to get home.

When his parents moved to Paris in 1953, Crown Prince Alexander was eight years old. They took rooms at the very comfortable Hôtel de Crillon. Later they called for their son to be sent to them. From New York City Alexander travelled alone on a Pan Am flight which he remembers as enormous with spacious beds to sleep in. It was very comfortable and the impressionable young boy travelled all by himself, in wonderment, hopeful about meeting up with his parents at the next destination which sounded remarkably as if it could be 'home'. Of course it was not, and again he was warehoused and barely ever saw them.

Restlessly his parents moved from Paris to Rome to Monte Carlo to the south of France, and endless other destinations; their life now a series of very deluxe hotels, perhaps the closest thing to palace life they could recreate. Everywhere they went they were taken care of financially by waves of loyalist monarchist Serb émigrés as well as newly-minted, super-rich friends. One example was a man named Paul-Louis Weiller who had stacked up a gigantic fortune betting against the war. Paul-Louis loved celebrities and collected them just as he collected sumptuous homes and beautiful objects and he would become significant in the lives of all sorts of homeless royals until his death at 100 in 1993. After the war, a whole new contingent had found wealth and while they may not all have had prestigious provenances these were mutually beneficial relationships. As my grandmother Princess Olga once said to me, 'Snobs? They're our best friends!' This was a very rare glimpse into her shrewder, slightly cynical side which generally was covered with soft layers of blue blood and good manners.

That Alexander's parents had no money and no home would have been lost on him while he was a child. All he knew was that when anyone asked him his nationality his reply was 'Yugoslav' despite the utter vagueness of what that meant. Serbian was not a language spoken in the home; they mostly spoke English when they were together, sometimes French. As a child, all he knew was that he was a member of this tiny tribe of three, and while he almost never saw his parents, he loved them and wanted more of their time than they could spare. He could not possibly fathom why this was the case, not until he was an adult, and then all he could do was respect them more for the hardships they endured and for his father's tenacity. Alexander is his father's son and that same tenacity is visible to this day. After all, here he is, learning as he goes, adapting as is his way, and with a deep commitment to a country that understands him only slightly less than he himself understands them. Patience, please!

During the late 1950s his parents moved from one European country to another, always in beautiful cities, always staying at fine hotels. A couple of times his parents bought homes of their own but it was generally a disaster as it was more than they could cope with. In truth, they preferred hotels, where you pick up a telephone and ask for things to be brought to you. After their childhoods in palaces filled with servants it was closer to what they knew. Sweetly, Alexander sees the silver lining in all this endless spinning about, and says, 'One benefit was I grew up seeing the greatest cities of the world and I saw a lot more than most kids my age.' Despite this, young Alexander was soon sent away by himself, sometimes to a family who might take him in for a summer, and later on to boarding schools. Crown Prince Alexander knew his parents loved him so this shunting around, while not welcome, was not taken as a rejection. On some deeper emotional level he knew this was not what he wanted. After all he enjoyed being with his parents on the rare occasions when they remembered they had a child, and invited him into their grown-up world. But it was fleeting and he always wanted more of it, even if he did not dare admit this to himself. Instead, he made excuses for them – they were busy, they had their hands full with trying to shift the machine of world politics in their favour. His parents not only believed in what they were doing, they took it deadly seriously – so how could he fault them? Yet he was a normal child who wanted to be in their company. Instead of losing his self-confidence or internalizing this discontent, young Alexander adapted; he made the best of things, he did not feel sorry for himself even if at times his life was lonely and confusing.

When his parents were in Paris, ten-year-old Alexander was sent to a family outside Geneva, in the district of Nyon, and there he spent an entire summer with someone else's family. To this day he does not remember who they were, only that he was happy, and that he enjoyed himself. He did not exactly miss his parents because this had become the norm, these open-ended stretches of time when he was not with them. If he thought about it at all, which no doubt he did, he loved his parents and felt bonded to them, and if his father said he was busy with matters of supreme importance – matters of State and working hard to get them all home – then all he could do was try not to add to the stress, but rather buck up, and do his part, if only by not being a nuisance. However – and this would not come to light quite yet – his mother Alexandra was increasingly emotionally destabilized. They had no fixed home, their future was debatable, their finances were uncertain, and one day this would manifest itself as chronic depression.

Alexander remembers one particular summer holiday: there was a lovely house near a gorgeous beach where every day he would play and swim, accompanied by his nanny. Each day he would beseech his father, 'Please come to the beach with me today, play with me!' And invariably his father would answer, 'I can't today, I'm meeting with this one and that one.' Everyone he mentioned was always titled and obviously important, and the meetings were referred to as essential. This went on day after day and finally young Alexander displayed a minimal flare of temper and said, 'How come you never meet with anyone normal? Like a Mr and Mrs?' King Peter may have felt a shard of guilt, he must have known he was letting down his son, but his life had never been his own. His childhood had been almost entirely one of duty and preparation for ruling a country. Caught off guard he retorted sharply to his young son, declaring it was not possible to break from his schedule. Alexander remembers this moment acutely; the glaring unfairness of it all, such a small request denied. It is possible Peter, too, felt a certain degree of recrimination, or perhaps he felt justified by the enormity of his mission. I hope the two sentiments intermingled, though the conflicts of his roles were no doubt confusing – a born leader and a father missing out on his son's childhood.

Starting around 1960, during his teenage years, Alexander began to notice his mother's bouts of depression. Even if he did not know the medical term for this condition, it was very obvious when she would become withdrawn, distant and far-away. She began to engage in hunger strikes. These episodes became glaringly evident and were as frightening for him as for his father.

All the endless moving around, the dislocation, the fixation on a future that seemed hopeless may have kept Peter's fire stoked, but his frailer wife wound down. As Peter remained stoic and stalwart in his goal to get back to Yugoslavia, Alexandra seems to have given up. As a Greek princess she had already experienced the terror and wrenching trauma of political exile and here it was again. It was possibly just too much. It was when Alexander was a teenager that he found out his father was a king. This news was bizarre, to say the least. Even more bizarre, he discovered that he, too, might be a king one day. The shock and confusion can only have inspired an avalanche of unanswerable questions.

Alexander distinctly remembers his father lamenting how he was homesick for Yugoslavia. Alexander says that his father frequently reminisced about his homeland, always mentioning how incredibly beautiful Yugoslavia was, how the air was sweet as honey, and how much he loved the mountains and forests of Šumadija, swimming in the lakes of Slovenia, and how he longed to get back. It seems Peter spent his whole adult life homesick for a country that had rejected him, ejected him, maligned him and still his love was undiminished. The genetic code of tribal yearning is indomitable.

All his adult life King Peter II was surrounded by both good and bad people, being fed copious amounts of good information and bad. While it helped sustain him, none of this ultimately got him any closer to his goal, a goal that at the time must have seemed improbable at best. Yet look at today, with Karageorgević family members trickling back to Serbia, one by one, feeling at home, and planting roots. It turns out Peter was not wrong and to me that is some consolation for his stark life of hope against all odds.

Alexander remembers his father never complained and he never gave up; rather he felt his life was predetermined and his energy and time were directed toward this inevitable return to Yugoslavia. Alexander clearly remembers his father frequently saying, 'Churchill let me down.' At other times he would add, interestingly, that Roosevelt had been more of an ally. Unfortunately the young Crown Prince Alexander never quizzed his father more deeply, it just was not the thing to do. Even though they were informal with each other, Alexander obviously felt inherent limits. Given that cosy lunches and dinners were rare, why would he choose to spend his time antagonizing his father?

For his teenage years Alexander was sent off to boarding schools: one year at the very well-known school Marie Jose, which he laughingly says he would not recommend to anyone, and then Le Rosey, also in Switzerland. Here he made friends he would keep for the rest of his life. The children of the extremely wealthy, the well-heeled, the displaced, the exiles and the off-spring of new money were all thrown together. The massive difference between him and the other school children was that when it came time for holidays and all his friends were fetched by parents, chauffeurs and limousines, or maybe even by helicopter, young Alexander had nowhere to go. Frequently he was left there, all alone, with the bare bones of the school staff.

In 1961 Queen Maria of Yugoslavia, King Alexander I's widow, died relatively young but emotionally drained. Alexander was sixteen when his grandmother died and he says he remembers her from his early childhood when he was taken to see her. He remembers her fondly, saying she was kind to him. Alexander says that these days he studies photographs of what she looked like before she died at sixty-one and he thinks possibly she must have been ill for a long time, because she looked so much older than her actual years. Alexander adds that he thinks despite the ravages of any disease she quite likely died of a broken heart and an impossibly stressful life over which she lost all control. After all, she was born a royal princess in a very grand palace in Romania. Her next step was as Queen Consort of Yugoslavia, bedecked with huge tiaras and a life of splendid receptions, and then the unforeseeable denouement – a terrible splitting of ends that would never weave back together. After her husband was shot to his death in the shocking assassination of 1934 in Marseilles, she was seemingly forcibly relocated to England in 1938 (conveniently before World War II began), and only permitted to bring with her the two youngest of her three sons. This, surely, was not her idea but one imposed upon her, again underscoring the fact her decisions were no longer hers to make. The widow queen would live out the remainder of her life as some sort of novelty to her neighbours in East Sussex in the south of England; entirely misunderstood, and probably keeping to herself, bereft as she was by now of all she once had known and believed in; reduced and humbled. Alexander's assessment that she died of a broken heart, a broken life, seems entirely plausible to me. According to Alexander his father, King Peter, never once spoke against his mother's decision to abandon him in Serbia in 1938, while moving permanently to England. Peter, who was all of fourteen years old and left behind with his cousins, would indisputably have been traumatized; that he never complained about it does not mean he did not experience any pain. Despite the difficulties, Peter would devote the remainder of his life to the dream of a return to Yugoslavia.

In 1966, when Alexander was twenty-one, his father explained to him how in 1947, when he was all of two years old, Marshal Tito's second in command wrote up a decree declaring him an enemy of the state and a threat to the country and stripped him of his Yugoslav nationality. Also included in this decree were his father Peter, his brothers Tomislav and Andrej, his Uncle Paul and all of Uncle Paul's children (meaning my grandparents and my uncles and my mother).

Many years later, and to her eternal credit, my courageous mother, Princess Elizabeth of Yugoslavia, demanded the sealed documents from the British government that proved the sanctioning of this expulsion. We are all very proud of the hard and dogged work my mother has managed to do against implacable bureaucracies to prove this was no mere rumour but rather a government-backed decision which made them all not only homeless, but nationless.

The reality was that for this suddenly nomadic family they not only had no home and no nationality, they were denied their cultural identity. King Peter and his consort Alexandra travelled around on passports issued from a royal Yugoslav embassy in Madrid. For Crown Prince Alexander, this lack of documentation became an ongoing and outlandish scene like something Voltaire might have written, tongue-in-cheek, whereby he had to apply for visas and special consideration to be permitted to travel at all. Crown Prince Alexander was a non-person.

The confirmation of this heavy-handed injustice infuriated the young Crown Prince Alexander. It meant that for the first fourteen years of his life he in fact had zero nationality. Instead of this news making him detest Yugoslavia for the harsh cruelty, Alexander says that it only helped to galvanize him and made him all the more determined to right this infuriating and gross unfairness. To me this shrieks of his Serb nature! Far from being cowed, he was inspired. Serbs are many things, but tenacity is a leading characteristic. Alexander clearly remembers speaking with his Uncle Paul (my grandfather) at my grandparents' home on the rue Scheffer and discussing this abominable situation. My grandfather fully agreed the treatment they received was appalling.

Around this time, when Alexander was twenty-one, his father told him for the first time about Oplenac: 'There is a place for us in Yugoslavia, it's a crypt, my space and your space are downstairs. You'll see one day.' This would have meant very little to Alexander until many years later when he visited the imposing family mausoleum. It is truly magnificent. On the first floor there are two enormous white blocks of marble, one for Karageorge and the other for King Peter I. Downstairs there are many spaces under marble mosaic archways, some now filled with bodies re-interred after being brought home from cemeteries abroad. My mother Princess Elizabeth of Yugoslavia is to be commended for her incredible work to repatriate the bodies of her parents and her older brother Nicholas – a man who died too young, long ago in an automobile accident. Impossible to overlook is the irony that while during our lifetimes the Karageorgević family has had mostly nowhere to live, they have always had somewhere to go once dead.

Alexander's father, King Peter, died in 1970 in Denver, Colorado after a failed liver transplant. The issue of where Peter should be buried was immediately a concern for his only child. Crown Prince Alexander asked his cousin HM Queen Elizabeth of the United Kingdom if his father could be buried beside his mother Queen Maria at Frogmore, the British royal cemetery and Queen Elizabeth agreed. But then a protracted fight began. Serbs in Chicago vociferously fought for the body to be buried at Libertyville, outside of Chicago, which led to a stalemate. This tug of war would last until the next century. In reality Alexander could do nothing without state assistance and it would be a long struggle before he had its backing. But he is not one to give up, and eventually he made it happen.

Alexander did not attend his father's funeral. However, his uncle Prince Andrej did. Not only did Andrej go to his brother's funeral in Denver, Colorado, but there he met the Mata Hari-like figure who would soon bewitch him and sweep him off his feet. Within minutes they were together in Las Vegas and they eventually married in 1974. After many years together in what some considered a bizarre union, Prince Andrej committed suicide in 1990. The local police department in Palm Springs declared it a suicide by carbon monoxide poisoning. It was a murky, tragic end to a sad life. Prince Andrej's three younger children, Lavinia, Vladimir and Dimitri, grew up mostly without him, living in Portugal with their mother. They must have had their own feelings of abandonment; no one emerged unscathed.

In 1970, shortly after the death of his father, when Crown Prince Alexander was twenty-five years old, his uncle Prince Tomislav asked to meet with him. The reason for this meeting was Prince Tomislav's notion that he should take the reins. Apparently Tomislav confronted his nephew, who was after all the rightful heir, and said, 'Why don't you sign the whole thing over to me?' He meant the succession to the throne of Yugoslavia. It is an unfortunate element in this family that scant acknowledgement is given to the rules of succession as they were laid down by King Peter I and then again by King Alexander I.

I think it is important to add that these issues were a product of the times. I am very glad to say that the current generation – my generation – meaning my cousin Prince Dimitri, myself, and Crown Prince Alexander's three sons, have no interest in any of this. We consider ourselves ordinary citizens, though of which country we are not entirely sure; it is a matter for each of us to deal with. However, we have no ambitions regarding thrones, and we wish only to live normal lives. I will say that we all labour under the extraordinary circumstances of a lack of clear cultural identity. The good news is that we can now examine those questions, and in our own time – and own ways – get to know our homeland of Serbia.

The 1970s were very different times, and Crown Prince Alexander's response was to be infuriated and reply, 'Absolutely no way!' To me, Alexander's reaction is entirely Serbian. The more I get to know him the more I see how much of a Serb he is, how much of a Serb I am, and that my mother and her explosive yet charming personality is also, quite simply, 100 per cent Serbian. Maybe none of us grew up knowing this and perhaps it is not even important, but I find it interesting, and a simple answer to nature versus nurture. Nature wins, hands down.

Sadly, though perhaps inevitably, that was the start of a break in their relationship and this would never be resolved. HRH Prince Tomislav died in 2000 in Topola where he had lived for the last few remaining years of his life. I remember meeting Tomislav when he lived on a farm in West Sussex in southern England, and I was at a boarding school nearby. I remember him as a tall and sombre man with huge cheekbones and muddy Wellington boots. I also remember that he was kind to me. His daughter Katarina was similar in age to me, and we easily became friends. Whatever tussles existed between the grown-ups were not at all apparent to me.

It is interesting to note that Karageorge himself held no stock in titles, in material wealth, in any form of frippery. He was a tough, shrewd man who was not seduced by showiness or shallow, superficial tripe. At odds with these characteristics, he believed in launching a dynasty that would survive the ages, and maybe most especially that it should outrank the rival Obrenović family. Karageorge did not fight for position but for freedom for himself and his fellow men. He was tough and relentless and murderous, but he was righteous. I believe if your goals are clear and just, your actions can be mitigated. Power for the sake of power is a useless self-aggrandizement. I have no proof if this conversation ever took place between Alexander and his uncle Tomislav, and if it did, I have no answers as to what Tomislav's motives might have been. What I do know is that Alexander's entire youth was spent watching his father's endless manoeuvring for restoration, so I can understand why it would have seemed inconceivable to him to simply hand things over, even if there was, in fact, nothing to hand over. As we all know, 100 per cent of nothing is still nothing.

In 1972, when Alexander was twenty-six years old, he married his first wife, the Brazilian Princess Maria da Glória of Orléans-Braganza. Their three sons, Peter, Philip and Alexander, were all born in the United States. Crown Prince Alexander always wanted a family of his own and he always intended to have children. With his new bride they lived in Brazil in a beautiful apartment. His in-laws had a giant spread north of Rio, and life was good for a time. As it happens, things ended amicably enough in 1985 and they got a divorce, Alexander's only concern being that his boys were going to be as unscathed as possible by this split. His own childhood had made him all the more sensitive to the needs of children. Sometimes people learn from their experiences and do not perpetuate the traumas. This is evolution at its finest and debunks, in my opinion, any room for blaming the past for the burdens of the present. It is up to each one of us to learn and to improve upon the past. This is a personal choice. The blame game is a pointless, self-serving dead end. Crown Prince Alexander is a good man with a kind and warm heart and despite his utterly bizarre childhood he has consciously decided to do better. Of course, if you speak to his sons, they will tell you that all they wanted was for things to go back to how they were before and to live with both their parents in a united family setting. Some scars are inevitable.

Alexander's childhood had been lonely and although he did all the right things and even married a princess who bore heirs, his real life was fairly normal, except that there was always this glinting fairy tale of a kingdom somewhere on the horizon, that might one day be his. If at thirty-nine years old Alexander knew anything for certain it was that he did not want to tackle life alone. As the ink dried on his divorce papers he met a Greek named Katherine Batis. They married in late 1985. Katherine had a son and a daughter from her first marriage and they did their best to blend their families. This, of course, is easier said than done. Alexander's children were pleased their father was happy, but if they could choose they would have waved a wand and put things back the way they had once been. A perfectly normal reaction.

On a slight tangent, when in 1986 I married my first husband, a Brit with Croat roots, my mother-in-law and my mother jointly planned a party to celebrate this union at someone's large London house. It just so happened I was under the weather from a bout of influenza and could barely walk, let alone make much sense. Nevertheless, my enterprising mother-in-law fed me handfuls of over-the-counter medications and ultimately I was ambulatory, though not necessarily aware of much that was going on. What I do remember is fairly fractured and dreamlike. The entrance hall was filled floor to ceiling with lavish gifts, including a very special present from none other than Paul-Louis Weiller, then in his late nineties, and not one to miss out on a royal-related event even if he was by now too weak to attend in person. The rest of the party surged under a tent in the back garden with a band and bars and waiters with trays of champagne and a great many guests. I was floating on air from all the medications I had consumed and not really participating except in a sort of out-of-body way. I remember an older man (keep in mind I was twenty-one at the time, so anyone over twenty-five seemed old to me) who approached and extended his hand for me to shake. He said, 'Congratulations on your wedding. It is my pleasure to meet you, Christina, I am the head of the family.' I had no idea who he was or what he was talking about. In my naturally glib way – and with the meds loosening my already naturally flippant tongue – I remember throwing my palm up face forward, Native American style, and replying, 'Hey, Chief!' This was my first encounter with Crown Prince Alexander. He was saying hello to me, but it went over my head and it would be many years before the two of us would reminisce about this little encounter and have a laugh over it.

Throughout his life Alexander always had a regular job. While he had a fancy title and this cartoonish possibility of 'ruling a country', he got on with normal life. He did not allow the vague promise that one day he would be King of a far-away country to interfere with the needs of modern-day life. Unlike his father, he put all that aside and prepared to deal with the reality at hand, to roll up his sleeves and participate in the world as it was, rather than how he might wish it to be, and to fulfil the requirements of earning a living.

Alexander worked in the insurance business, first in Chicago and then in Virginia, always relocating for work, but like his father he kept an eye on Yugoslavia and the state of affairs politically. This was simply in his blood. However, over the years, when people would ask him, 'Don't you want to be King?' he would always answer, 'King of what?' During his lifetime, Yugoslavia was always staunchly communist and then, after Tito's death, it devolved into the mess that was the Milošević dictatorship. But with this new regime came the first flicker of possibility, and he knew it. Change, regardless of which direction it might go, was possible.

In 1989 Alexander was forty-three years old and of course he had been watching the political situation in Yugoslavia all his adult life. Even though things had seemed impossible regarding returning, suddenly shifts and schisms were appearing. Everywhere he had ever lived Alexander says he felt at home – he adapted. Yet the instant it became a possibility to get into Yugoslavia he jumped at it. He remembers he was in San Francisco having talks with expatriate Serbs and other supporters when the notion of returning to the homeland became more of an actuality. It was as if the flakes in the snow globe had finally settled, and there before his eyes was the slim chance of a door cracking open, the entry his father had spent a lifetime believing in and searching for.

By late 1989 Alexander allowed himself a certain degree of optimism about what he saw as viable changes, suggesting the first small step to his potential return. Immediately this option captivated his imagination. He was drawn magnetically, not from ego, but from some far deeper primal instinct. This was his home, even though he had never so much as stepped foot in the country. Despite a lifetime abroad, with seemingly no hope of ever returning – still deemed an enemy of the State – he started to plan. He held conferences including one in Athens. Rather cleverly, he shuffled the squabbling delegates around until they began to make connections and started to work together.

For the next two years Alexander continued, even more determinedly, to meet with supporters as they all watched a changing Yugoslavia shattering and reconfiguring after the death of Tito and then splintering further under the insane dictatorship of Milošević. Out of nowhere, suddenly Alexander had a conviction that he could, indeed, fulfil his father's dreams. The completely impossible had gradually become a reality.

With this unified support behind him he made his journey to Yugoslavia. This initial trip to the fatherland was in 1991 and for the first time in his life he did not need any kind of passport because his fans and followers swarmed the airport enthusiastically and joyously greeted him. This was a tremendous welcome after two generations of waiting and watching and analysing, of doubts mingling with a burgeoning determination. Yet he prevailed and he was in his own country. On that first visit he attempted to get into the grounds of his father's home at the palace complex of Dedinje, but guards with guns held him back at the gates. This was less a humiliation than a rock-solid reason to return, to be better prepared another time.

His three sons, however, did not share his enthusiasm. They were terrified their father could be assassinated. All they wanted was for life to go back to the cosy time of their childhood. While they were uncertain about the very concept of Serbia, at the same time, when they visited the country they felt a kinship. Even if they could not necessarily put a name to their feelings, a connection existed. DNA is a powerful divining rod.

When Alexander returned to Yugoslavia for the second time in 2000, he and Zoran Djindjic worked together. In 2001, when Djindjic – as the newly-elected prime minister – and Alexander were celebrating in the prime minister's office in the centre of Belgrade, Djindjic impulsively said, 'How did you get here, do you have a car?' Alexander replied, 'Yes I have a car, it's right out front.' Djindjic said, 'Let's go storm Dedinje and take it over!' Alexander laughed, and said, 'Calm down! I tried that once before and I was met with guns. Let's do things pragmatically.'

The 1990s were a bloody shambles for everyone, and many good people lost their lives. Civil war raged and Bosnia exploded with ancient resentments which were immediately usurped by the Western military complex in the name of liberty and human rights. The West backed the Bosnian Muslims, creating a white-wash by renaming this civil war 'ethnic cleansing' until it was not possible for a single Serb to stay in his ancestral homeland. The West supported the Muslims of Sarajevo to the detriment of all other nationalities, neatly establishing a fresh hotbed for extremists. Again, later in 1999, displaying the West's gross disregard for history, they smashed Kosovo in the name of ethnicities of which they had zero understanding. People of all ethnicities died and 700,000 Serbs were relocated permanently to Belgrade, a city already bursting at the seams.

During the war years, Alexander and Katherine had nothing to do but wait it out, watch and pray. The American government, and frontwoman Madeleine Albright (who is not only of Czechoslovakian descent, but had once lived in Belgrade as a child, which one hoped would have given her a modicum of understanding, though evidently not), bombed Serbia's capital of Belgrade, a heavily populated city, behind the mighty shield of NATO. To this day the buildings hit by the bombs sag with enormous broken slabs of cement, and shrubs and trees grow out of the cracks. Secretary Albright green-lighted the dropping of many thousands of bombs filled with spent uranium. Now much of the population of Serbia is riddled with a variety of cancers.

By the end of the 1990s, Serbia, bereft of alliances with its neighbours and now economically reduced and punished by UN sanctions, was exhausted. It was at this time my mother moved there. She bought herself a home in the centre of town, she learned the language and she became justifiably enormously popular. No matter that she was not living in a palace, my mother was home to stay – and I had never before seen her so content, at ease and happy. She set to work rehabilitating her father's besmirched name and working to restore ownership of snatched family property.

In 2000 Crown Prince Alexander and Crown Princess Katherine also returned to Serbia. They toured the country and when Katherine saw the condition of the hospitals she said, 'I have to get involved.' Today Crown Princess Katherine has raised millions of dollars and arranged for ambulances and cars and medical equipment to be donated all over the country. In 2001 they moved into the palace of Dedinje.

The Crown Prince's great ally and friend Zoran Djindjic would become mayor of Belgrade in 1997 and prime minister of Serbia from 2001 to 2003. Tragically, Djindjic was murdered in 2003 – shot in the head in broad daylight in the centre of Belgrade. This was a great loss for the country and on a personal level also for Crown Prince Alexander and Crown Princess Katherine who enjoyed his support. Nevertheless, they continue to cooperate and to work with whatever government is elected. While there is no real consensus on my family living in Serbia, or owning anything that once belonged to their parents or grandparents, I believe it is Alexander's great honour and pleasure to fulfil his father's greatest wish: that the Karageorgević family lives in its homeland, however unclear the future may be.

When I ask Alexander about his father he defends him. He says, 'My father was seventeen years old. What would you have done in his shoes? Do you expect him to be a political genius at seventeen?' Alexander says that his father was someone who considered and measured every word he said. He did not speak hastily, he was thoughtful, and because of this trait many misunderstood him, including his tutor Cecil Parrott who thought him a distracted student. Alexander asks who at the age of seventeen could run a country as complicated as Yugoslavia in the 1930s when the world was exploding and conflicted by impossible ideologies. Alexander is very proud of his father for going on to study at Cambridge University, where he made many friends. Peter, despite being dealt a very strange hand, always took his life's mission extremely seriously. It might have seemed delusional at the time, but now everyone is coming home. Peter was not wrong, he was just ahead of his time. I salute him.

Crown Prince Alexander remembers that when he was in the company of his parents, throughout his very unusual childhood, they were sweet with him, they were informal and relaxed and they were kind. He says he knew he was loved; unlike, say, my grandfather – Uncle Paul as Alexander calls him – who was abandoned emotionally and literally by his biological parents. Alexander not only loved and respected his parents, he felt their love for him. Meanwhile, this generous and sensitive largesse was entirely in conflict with the repeated infrequency with which he saw them and the extended lengths of time between visits. Even when he was with them, he was separate from them, living mostly with a nanny. Sometimes they were in separate countries. The greatest balm of childhood is this myopia; whatever one's experience it is not until later, when there is a greater frame of reference, that one can make comparisons. This single fact insulated Alexander – he would say 'inoculated' him – from the pain of neglect.

The contradiction was that his parents did love him, and from a sincere sense of duty they did not throw him to the wolves. At the same time, they never made him a priority. His father, King

Peter II, was entirely swept up with his fixation on how to get home to his kingdom, and his wife Alexandra was a fragile lady who dutifully endorsed her husband's quest until it cracked her innate fragility, and reduced her ability to cope. No doubt she loved her son, but as Alexander will tell you, this was only apparent when they seemed – every once in a while – to remember his existence and to have maybe a lunch here or a dinner there. Then, once more, he was sent away when his father had important meetings to manage, always with influential types who were equally determined to see him restored to his position as King of Yugoslavia. The young Crown Prince was yet another piece of shrapnel caught in the endless cycle of collateral damage that was the product of the exiled royals. No one lived a normal life; no one would have even known what that meant.

His parents travelled endlessly, restlessly, in search of a place to live, regardless of their lack of funds or shaky status or lack of legal passports. All the while the little Crown Prince followed behind, summoned, though never really invited to stay, only brought along as a piece of luggage, usually the last to join and then almost at once sent off somewhere.

The family was supported by loyalist émigrés and the eccentric rich; for example vastly wealthy individuals like Paul-Louis Weiller, a French Jew with a penchant for the suddenly impoverished royals forever washing up on the shores of Paris, the south of France and the like. Weiller is well known for providing houses and funding for many of these displaced people with their fabulous backgrounds and empty bank accounts, rendered suddenly homeless, penniless and adrift. He was a major factor behind the scenes with enormous wealth of his own. In return, he enjoyed the company of these grateful well-mannered nomads and each benefitted in their own way. But there were many others also supporting these great ships that had run aground, else how could they have lived? None of them were suitable for regular employment, add to that the notion they all had their sights trained on returning to their respective homelands, no matter how unlikely. They were in a state of extended emotional limbo, and some of them lived the remainder of their lives with a rigid belief and concept that was entirely at odds with the changing times and the new reality of a modernizing world.

Since 2001, after careful negotiations between my cousins and the magnanimity of the Federation of Serbia, HRH Crown Prince Alexander and Crown Princess Katherine have resided at the palace complex of Dedinje. They meet with dignitaries, they invite busloads of orphans to tea parties, and they devote themselves daily to public causes for the betterment of a country that is getting to know them just as they are getting acquainted with it. It is a symbiotic exchange that is earnest, heartfelt, long overdue and yet at the same time riven with complications. My mother for her part is always busy looking for ways to help restore what she believes is rightfully hers and, at the same time, throwing her energy behind what she believes she can do for this country. She has set up foundations, and she has raised money and awareness. My mother is a fighter!

Both my mother and her cousin the Crown Prince have deeply emotional ties to the country of Serbia. Right or wrong, their actions are driven in great part by this deep-rooted passion, this need to fulfil and redeem the stolen lives of their parents. I see them as the bridge between what was and what will be. The future for the Karageorgević family is bright because my generation is less conflicted by emotion and more motivated by enthusiasm. My mother and Alexander are fighting the battle of past ghosts, righting the wrongs inflicted on them and their own immediate antecedents. The future, however, is another story.

While the family is looking to regain the possessions ripped from them, they are in no way seeking retribution for the past. An example of this shift in perspective, this move from revenge for the unjustness of the past to humanity for the shared collateral damage of the present day, is evident in a particularly moving incident when Crown Prince Alexander found out that Tito's widow was living in a huge house near the Dedinje Palace. She was living in total darkness because her electricity had been switched off for failure of payment. A lesser man – a bitter man – would have rejoiced at this slight by fate. Instead, Crown Prince Alexander at once made arrangements directly with the Serbian government on her behalf to have the electricity and heat immediately switched back on. Crown Prince Alexander is new to this country, relatively speaking, but he is Serbian through and through. He has a heart of gold and his natural inclination is to do good.

Rather astoundingly it was not until 2008 that the ban was officially lifted and members of the Karageorgević family were legally welcome to return without fear of being met with a bullet. Now that Serbia was opening its creaky doors to him and the family, Alexander became evermore intent on relocating his dead parents' bodies to the family crypt, Oplenac. Fox News invited the Crown Prince to be interviewed regarding his intentions and when the Fox newscaster asked him, 'Why must your father's remains go to the family crypt? Why is this such a big deal for you?' Alexander's reply was, 'When your decorated American soldiers die where are they buried?' The Fox anchorman replied,

'Arlington Cemetery', to which Alexander hotly said, 'Exactly! It's the same for my family.' For whatever reason this segment was never aired.

In 2013, my mother – after years of tenacity – convinced the necessary authorities to assist her with transferring the bodies of her parents and her brother Nicholas from a cemetery in Switzerland to the family crypt. This was hugely significant as it set a precedent and was welcomed by Serbs everywhere. It was time, and I congratulate her for her tireless efforts in making this come to fruition. I love my mother very much and I appreciate that her life was extremely unconventional. From a young and tender age she experienced upheaval and chaos and she has coped with it all with a fierce strength and a sense of humour. My mother has leapt over huge hurdles and overcome struggles. I am so proud to see her hard work pay off and to see her home in Serbia where she deserves to be. Princess Elizabeth is loved in Serbia and she is never shy about rolling up her sleeves and getting involved whenever the need crops up. Whether it be to raise money for orphanages or flood victims, my mother is repeatedly at the forefront doing whatever she can to help. She is Serbian through and through, and she is my hero.

Never one to compromise what he believes in, Crown Prince Alexander was next to transfer the earthly remains of his parents and his uncle Andrej to their proper resting place at Oplenac. This was achieved in 2014 and all Serbs agree this was an important and noteworthy achievement.

As I speak with my cousin in the blue and gold sitting room of the fantastically beautiful Dedinje Palace, with a view through immense elegant windows of manicured gardens filled with statues and beyond that dark forests and hillocks, my cousin remarks on a shocking and poignant reality. His grandfather King Alexander I, the visionary who designed, conceived and built Dedinje, only lived there for five years: from 1929 when the complex was completed until his assassination in 1934. His father, King Peter II, spent only twelve years of his life in this home: from 1929 until he was deposed by the conspiracies of the British and the Serbian opposition in 1941. Crown Prince Alexander and Crown Princess Katherine have been in residence since 2001.

EPILOGUE

I HAVE COME TO THE END OF MY QUEST. I HAVE LEARNED about my ancestors and I am impressed by their exploits. I consider it a great honour to be related to them and it is my sole desire to do my part, whatever that may be, to contribute to this beautiful country and its rather fascinating and unique people. Like my grandfather, I have a natural inclination toward the arts and I will follow those instincts where they take me, but always with the intention of directing my services to the benefit of Serbs and Serbia. What an extraordinary privilege. The more I delved into the past, the more I clarified who I am and what I am. From this examination, I can better understand my Serbian mother.

My mother was born in the palace of Beli Dvor, a princess at a time when the Yugoslav monarchy existed and as a result of this she was invested from the start with a feeling of pride and certainty, both in her Yugoslav nationality and her religion, which is Serbian Orthodox, and the essence of her very identity. As it turned out, she would need these tools. They provided her with an inner strength that she would repeatedly rely on when her life crashed into unimaginable tumult. Right before her fifth birthday everything she had once known was over. Her life entered a stretch of insecurity in Africa, followed by her maturing into a young lady with a title but no homeland. She was faced with the protocols of the past and yet had to cope with the modernizing world of the late 1950s. Her life prior to returning to Serbia was supported by this unique confidence in her heritage; it was an endless series of changes, from marriages, to domiciles, even to her own name. She was born HRH Princess Elizabeth of Yugoslavia and today she is Jelisaveta Karageorgević. But her earliest years on Earth were the fuel she would need to see her through a highly unconventional life and finally propel her back home to Belgrade, the city of her birth, where she lives today.

I am Russian Orthodox. I was baptized by a Russian Orthodox priest in a private chapel at my grandfather's Villa Demidoff. I was born in New York City and raised mostly in the UK. My mother is half-Greek and half-Serbian and was christened Serbian Orthodox. What does that make me? Half-American and half-Serbian, an amalgamation of worlds of which I am proud. The more I have learned about who I am the more at ease I have felt. I see now that I am lucky, and for that I am grateful.

My closest relative in terms of friendship is my cousin HRH Prince Dimitri of Yugoslavia. If there were still a royal family in Italy and the laws of succession changed as they have today in most monarchies to favour the eldest regardless of gender, he would be the next King of Italy as his mother was the eldest child of the last King, Umberto. We have been close friends since we were tiny children. Dimitri is, quite naturally, the family historian and he has diligently steered my efforts to compile my family story. Dimitri also has an artist's eye and talent. His twin brother Michel claims the same. I would say my sister Catherine got the looks, and I got the writing gene. We all seem to have survived the storm in our own ways, somewhat financially reduced and yet emotionally wealthy with artistic talents and unassailable determination. I see us all as tough, though in different ways. I see us as unswayed by compromise and unmotivated by convention. The more I learn about Serbia and Serbians the more I see how Serbian we are and for this I am inordinately relieved and proud. An answer at last.

Deep down the people who cared the most – King Peter II, his son Crown Prince Alexander, my grandfather Prince Paul, my grandmother Olga, my uncle Alexander and my mother Elizabeth – were the ones who most deeply cared to live in Serbia. I am delighted to see the start of the migration of Karageorgević family members coming home. It has been a long time. My sister Catherine Oxenberg, in her capacity as an actress on an American television show in 1984, was the first to return to Serbia, albeit not in person but rather as a character on a show named, ironically enough, *Dynasty*.

Next was my mother in 1992, concealed behind her married name of Mrs Manuel Ulloa (her third husband and a former prime minister of Peru); she entered the country for the first time since the coup of 1941. She insisted on visiting Beli Dvor, the house where she was born. When she got there she engaged in conversation with a very old man working as a gardener, and amazingly it turned out he had worked there since before World War II. When she introduced herself he broke down crying. My mother knew right then and there that one day, as soon as it was legally possible, she would return to live in her homeland, and she would stay. In 2000, the Federal Republic of Serbia slowly began to change its official policy toward Karageorgević family members and ever since we have been trickling in.

Since I have been in Serbia people ask me, 'Why now? What do you want? Do you want to be Queen?' And I say I came to take a look, but now I want to stay. The more I see the more I know I am not interested in, or seduced by, any desire to be a queen, even if it were on the table, which it is not. Meanwhile, I do have a natural inclination to be a part of Serbia in some capacity, unofficial, official, whatever. I already love the country and I want to give whatever I can. This is an instinctive response which I'm loving as I've never felt that way anywhere else. It feels like a huge relief to me, this sense of belonging without the need of any return on my investment. I don't want or need anything, yet I very much want to give. I like this feeling. It is new to me and entirely genuine.

Recently, my life and perspective changed again when I had the pleasure of meeting the three sons of Crown Prince Alexander: Peter, Philip and Alexander. Typical of my family, I never so much as knew of their existence. Equally they knew nothing about me, yet the minute we met we were friends. Like me, they are interested in this country, they are keen to spend time in Serbia and learn not just the language but also the culture, the traditions; to visit the land and meet the people, though not in any sort of formal capacity. None of us have any ambition or desire for a hand in politics or even the restoration of the monarchy. We come as regular citizens with open eyes and open hearts and all of us have acknowledged a definite and tangible connection. Unlike our parents who have been motivated by emotions, we are propelled by enthusiasm and curiosity. It is our pleasure and our privilege to discover that we are, along with various other strains, very Serbian.

I asked Hereditary Prince Peter Karageorgević a few questions, with no expectations of how he would answer, or even how he would feel about being asked such questions, nor to what degree he would choose to reveal himself. What I discovered was a man with no trouble speaking the truth, shooting right from the hip, glossing over nothing and opening up with an endearingly humble honesty. I immediately felt love for this cousin who, up until six months ago, I never knew existed. It is with tremendous joy I discover my family and Peter and his brothers have my full admiration. Through Peter's answers I see our similarities and also our genetic link to Karageorge.

In brief, the facets that best describe Hereditary Prince Peter Karageorgević are a composite of humility, humour and honesty. Along with his younger twin brothers, Philip and Alexander, who were raised far from Serbia, he is used to living a normal, private life. My generation all feel the same in our stepping through the looking glass into Serbia, a place that is at once new to us, and yet with which we feel an indescribable connection.

Peter was extremely gracious and agreed to an interview on what it means to be a hereditary prince in a country he is only just familiarizing himself with, where the monarchy itself is a hot issue. Peter tells me that while he is enjoying this foray into Serbian culture and getting to know Belgrade for the intriguing, lively city that it is, he has no ambition to elbow his way to the front of any crowd, or melt beneath the hot scrutiny of press and paparazzi. Instead, he says he prefers to reserve the right to maintain his privacy as he learns about the country and its people, 'in my own time, and on my own terms.' Peter and his brothers Philip and Alexander feel the same way and are not interested in being in the spotlight. However, this does not mean they would not like to help and get involved. They just want to do it without the harsh scrutiny of media attention. Quite evidently Peter does seem very much in the mould of Karageorge, who was famously quoted as saying: 'Not into titles, but into deeds!' Peter and his brothers are true Karageorgevićs! I can think of no higher compliment.

Q: When you visit Serbia do you feel a connection with the country or the people?

A: I don't really feel a connection with anyone or anything, anywhere. But I do really enjoy a lot of the aspects and traits of the people, and Belgrade is a great city. I haven't travelled to many places outside of the city yet – when I have done it's only been to official events and always surrounded by large crowds. I despise large crowds, let alone being the focal point of said large crowd.

Q: Do you have any interest in having a second home here? (Not the palace – a place of your own.)

A: That would be nice. I would like to get to know the country and people better on my own and in my own time / terms.

Q: If I told you there is a huge amount of land in the Šumadija district (around Topola) that belongs to our family would you have any interest in getting some of it and maybe building a summer home there? It's a spectacularly beautiful area.

A: Of course. But at the same time I don't know if I deserve anything like that. There are a lot of people going through some serious problems who deserve to be taken care of.

Q: Do you feel like you want to do something helpful for Serbia? Open a business, create a cultural exchange of some sort, be an unofficial ambassador?

A: Yes that would be nice. But I hate being in any sort of spotlight, if I could help without being the focus of any media
attention that would be ideal.

Q: How do you feel about the future of the royal family in
Serbia? [When I posed my final question to him about the
future of the royal family in Serbia, he replied with a quote
from Thomas Paine.]

A: 'One of the strongest natural proofs of the folly of hereditary right in kings is that nature disapproves it, otherwise
she would not so frequently turn it into ridicule by giving
mankind an ass for a lion.'   Thomas Paine, *Common Sense*.

∽

Dimitri and I saw pages written in our grandmother's hand,
which we recognized effortlessly. We saw, with our own eyes,
the letter from King Alexander to our grandfather with the
instructions for succession, the fabled letter and the now opened
envelope with the broken red wax seal; something we had heard
about all our lives, family lore come full circle. There it was
along with a multitude of other gripping information. Dimitri
is yet to visit Serbia, disinclined just as I was to come as a mere
tourist. He assisted me invaluably with private family history in
the compilation of this book, and the drawing of the family tree.

When I began this book, which was really only a compilation
of all the family members from Karageorge to the present day,
my expectation was to wrap it all up with a reference to both
my mother and Crown Prince Alexander, and to show by their

actions that despite a very bumpy ride, everyone was home with the best of intentions. I thought my story would end with my mother's generation and all her good works in Serbia, selflessly motivated by love and sentiment; and also the good works of Crown Prince Alexander and his complicated position as the head of the family.

Then, however, I met the three sons of Crown Prince Alexander, and irreversibly my thinking changed. I was not only impressed, I was relieved. I made a point to single each one of them out and ask many questions, I wanted to know who they were and what they thought. In truth, I expected to find them nostalgic and sentimental regarding this confused past. But it was quite the opposite. What I encountered was the closing of a loop on a story that began over 200 years ago. I met three gentlemen who have all of Karageorge's humble views and none of the pretensions of the muddled thinking of some of his descendants.

The true DNA of Karageorge is a stringent belief in equality, fearlessness, justice, and fairness; a sense of fun, humility and thoughtfulness. Throughout his descendants these traits are easily discernible, despite a couple of instances where vanity or greed may have jagged the path. The true Karageorgević traits though are clean and pure and good. If I was offered the choice of being a princess or a Karageorgević, hands down I choose being a Karageorgević. It is an honour and a privilege!

Now that I learn about Serbs I know for sure all those traits I agonized over and painstakingly examined are pure Serb – my fearlessness, my love of play, my artistic temperament, my swift temper, my strength and, ultimately, my passions. This is all pure Serb and I could not be more delighted to find this out.

Furthermore, and more importantly, when I met the three sons of Crown Prince Alexander I was amazed to find all three of them are devoid of vanity. In this they are as close to Karageorge in temperament as one could be. They want neither titles, special consideration, nor to be in the public spotlight. It is my great privilege to be part of the team that I consider to be the future of the Karageorgević family.

I don't need to be a princess to feel special. Far more important to me – and far more valuable – is to be a Karageorgević. I feel such pride in this; I treasure it, I cherish my new family and my new life, and I humbly and gratefully accept this extraordinary gift of great good luck. I swear to uphold my good name and to do my best, whatever that may be.

Hello Serbia, we are pleased to meet you!
Поздрав, Србијо. Задовољство нам је да вас упознам
Zdravo, Srbijo, drago nam je što smo se upoznali!

ACKNOWLEDGEMENTS

THANKS TO THE EXEMPLARY DILIGENCE OF THE POWERS that be at Columbia University, New York City (in particular Tanya Chebotarev, curator of the Bakhmeteff Archive of Russian and East European History) my grandfather Paul's personal correspondence has been immaculately preserved in dozens of well-marked folders. My cousin HRH Prince Dimitri of Yugoslavia and I – and my dear friend Henry Bisharat – spent a day examining these documents. This was a transformative experience.

In Serbia, a thank you to my genius editor Professor Čedomir Antić, inspired publisher Dejan Papić of Laguna, and my friend Zeljka Milanović. Of course a very special thank you to my friend and fixer Veljko Stojiljković, also *moja majka* Rada Stojiljković for both love and chicken soup. My greatest thanks to Aleksandar Sale Jovanović, aka 'Sir Oliver', Serbia's premier political commentator. My gratitude also to new friends for life, Igor and Ivan Stojanović. My eternal thanks to the exceptionally talented Serb poet Miloš Mitrović for some very sensitive advice.

In the United States I would like to thank my very excellent friend, former US State Department diplomat, Henry Bisharat, for his tireless, diligent and patient assistance with one trillion edits and historical details that only he could have found! And also to my many friends including Vanessa Noel for her tenderness and shelter, and my fairy godmother Mona Sadler for so very much.

In Key West I am grateful to all those who supported me in so many ways during this past year, not least of whom was Mr Christopher Robinson who re-read my endless revisions. A very special thank you to my darling beloved 'King Lear' the legendary visionary David Wolkowsky, aka the King of Key West. Also my very first real live Serb pal, Rasko Aksentijević, who admonished me the day I met him regarding my utter ignorance of all things Serbian, and is partially responsible for opening my eyes to this beautiful history. Also former Key West City Manager and son of one of Serbia's most important Chetniks, Mr Bogdan Vitas. In Key West, Marko Miladonović and Adrija Vuković provided invaluable assistance with Serbian translations.

And thank you to those who gave me my first introduction to historical research, particularly the late Hugh Montgomery-Massingberd and Hugo Vickers.

A most especial thank you to Leigh Honey Vogel who every time I phoned and whined and declared I could not write another word, simply said, 'You have to.' Thank you, Leigh, for keeping me going all the way to the end. I love you always.

My deep and humble gratitude to all my relatives who supported my quest for knowledge and answered my many questions, in particular my cousin Prince Dimitri of Yugoslavia, and my aunt Princess Barbara of Liechtenstein and Yugoslavia, my cousins TRH Crown Prince Alexander and Crown Princess Katarina of Serbia, Hereditary Prince Peter Karageorgević, Prince Philip and Alexander Karageorgević. My everlasting love to my late grandparents, Apapa and Amama (Prince Paul and

Princess Olga), who were the first to inspire me to examine our uniquely interesting past and our extensive family. And most importantly my inspiration, my hero and my heart – my mother Princess Elizabeth of Yugoslavia (Jelisaveta Karageorgević).

AUTHOR'S NOTE

MUCH OF THE MATERIAL I HAVE GATHERED HERE I FOUND on the Internet. Some facts are taken directly and for this I make no apologies. My sole objective and only desire is to collect the correct information and tell the story as it should be, rather than pretending to reveal previously unknown secrets which in any case would be beyond my capacity, especially since I am learning most of this for the first time. My goal here is not to spring on you, dear reader, some sensational news, but rather to compile and share this story as best I can if only to have it all in one place. I hope to make sense of what has always been confusing, or perhaps to bring home the dispersed threads of my very own Slavic family members, scattered all over the Earth. It is so sad to me that some of us have never met, have never even heard of one another. Perhaps, deep down, this is what I hope this book will help to correct.

For the purposes of research I have relied on friends, family, diaries, photo albums, books, newspaper clippings and the Internet. Here is the story as best as I could cobble it together. Please forgive the inevitable errors. I do not consider this a comprehensive nor definitive history and anyone with more correct information is encouraged to write me: kristina@kristinaoxenberg.com.